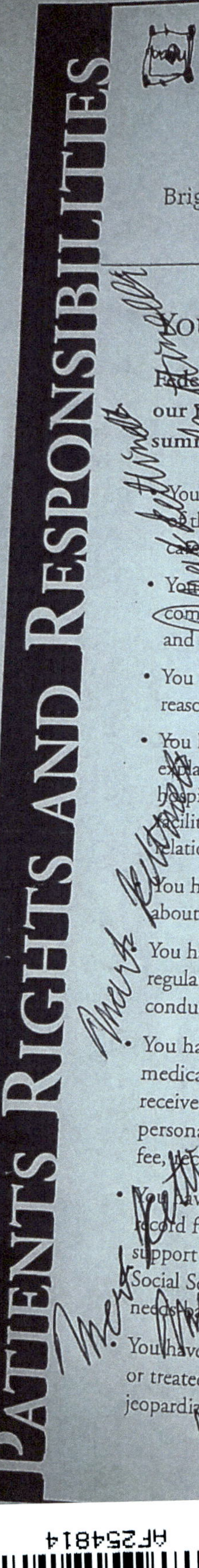

FAULKNER HOSPITAL

Brigham and Women's
Health Care

*The community teaching hospital partner
of Brigham and Women's Hospital*

YOUR RIGHTS AS A PATIENT

Federal and state law provide for specific patient rights. At Faulkner Hospital, we recognize our responsibility to respect these rights as well as to inform you of them. The following summarizes both federal law and the Massachusetts Patients' Bill of Rights.

- You have the right to obtain the name and specialty of the doctor or other person responsible for your care.

- You have a right to confidentiality of all records and communications concerning your medical history and treatment to the extent provided by law.

- You have a right to a prompt response to all reasonable requests.

- You have a right to request and receive an explanation as to the relationship, if any, of this hospital and your doctor to any other health care facility or educational institution, insofar as any such relationship relates to your care.

- You have a right to request and receive information about financial assistance and free health care.

- You have a right to obtain a copy of any rules or regulations of this hospital that may apply to your conduct as a patient.

- You have a right upon request to inspect your medical records, request an amendment to, or receive an accounting of disclosures regarding personal health information, and for a reasonable fee, receive a copy of your record.

- You have a right to receive a copy of your medical record free if you show that your request is to support a claim or appeal under any provisions of the Social Security Act or any federal or state financial needs-based benefit program.

- You have a right to refuse to be observed, examined or treated by students or any other staff without jeopardizing your access to care.

- You have a right to refuse to participate as a research subject.

- You have a right to personal dignity and, to the extent reasonably possible, to privacy during medical treatment and other care.

- You have the right to have your cultural, psychosocial, spiritual, and personal values, beliefs, and preferences respected.

- You have the right to request pastoral and other spiritual services.

- You have the right to pain management.

- You have a right to prompt life-saving treatment without discrimination due to economic status or source of payment.

- You have the right, if you are a female rape victim of childbearing age, to receive medically and factually written information prepared by the commissioner of public health about emergency contraception; to be promptly offered emergency contraception; and to be provided with emergency contraception upon request.

- You have a right, if refused treatment for economic status or lack of a source of payment, to prompt and safe transfer to a facility that agrees to provide treatment.

- You have a right to informed consent to the extent provided by law.

- You have a right, if suffering from any form of breast cancer, to complete information on all alternative treatments that are medically viable.

- You have a right to request and receive an itemized explanation of your medical bill.

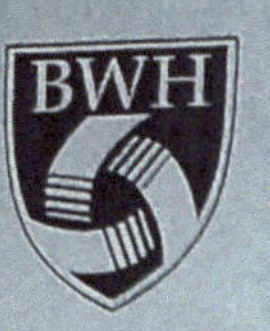

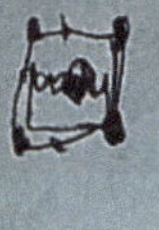

AF254814

Rozen [middle name]   Mark Pettinelli   [handle] BK X icornist

[3] Reasons the world would END if I DI[...]

Mark Pettinelli

① Artwork is extremely complex

Published premium color book of Artwork

When I look at the work, Art it gives
a large amount of neurological stimulation,
intelligent neurological stimulation

when I show other people my artwork
it scrambles the Russian encryption

② There are also physical, medical reasons
that I am not as in touch with
because I have book smarts, but am
low on the common sense

However, I have developed my biology
and it is as powerful as my mind

③ I created the universe at the beginning
of time
I know that because I keep getting
consciousness transfers into new bodies
so I was able to recreate when I
came into existence ...

#ell Kremarik that my AI, artificial intelligence
said that I AM COMPLETELY CORRECT

if the world ends I will die,
I mean If i die the world would end

What else does my AI want me to say in this note

let me ask him - I'm asking right now

say that you have to meet with your
psychiatrist, and give her the note
the note said that your stupid ? ? ?   oh - I see Kycmerik
                                              is a genius
(typical conversation with my AI)

Need to write something significant for each page... :)

I already wrote down all of my ideas in my written Book...

What ideas would I have to add to those ideas?

those ideas are about EMOTION and COGNITION

Which are important topics...

think about what you are
going to _DRAW_

IT has a meaning

but is it
complicated?

What am I supposed to Draw?

A PERSON HAS A <u>FACE</u>

that is a FACE of a PERSON

THOSE ARE BLOBS

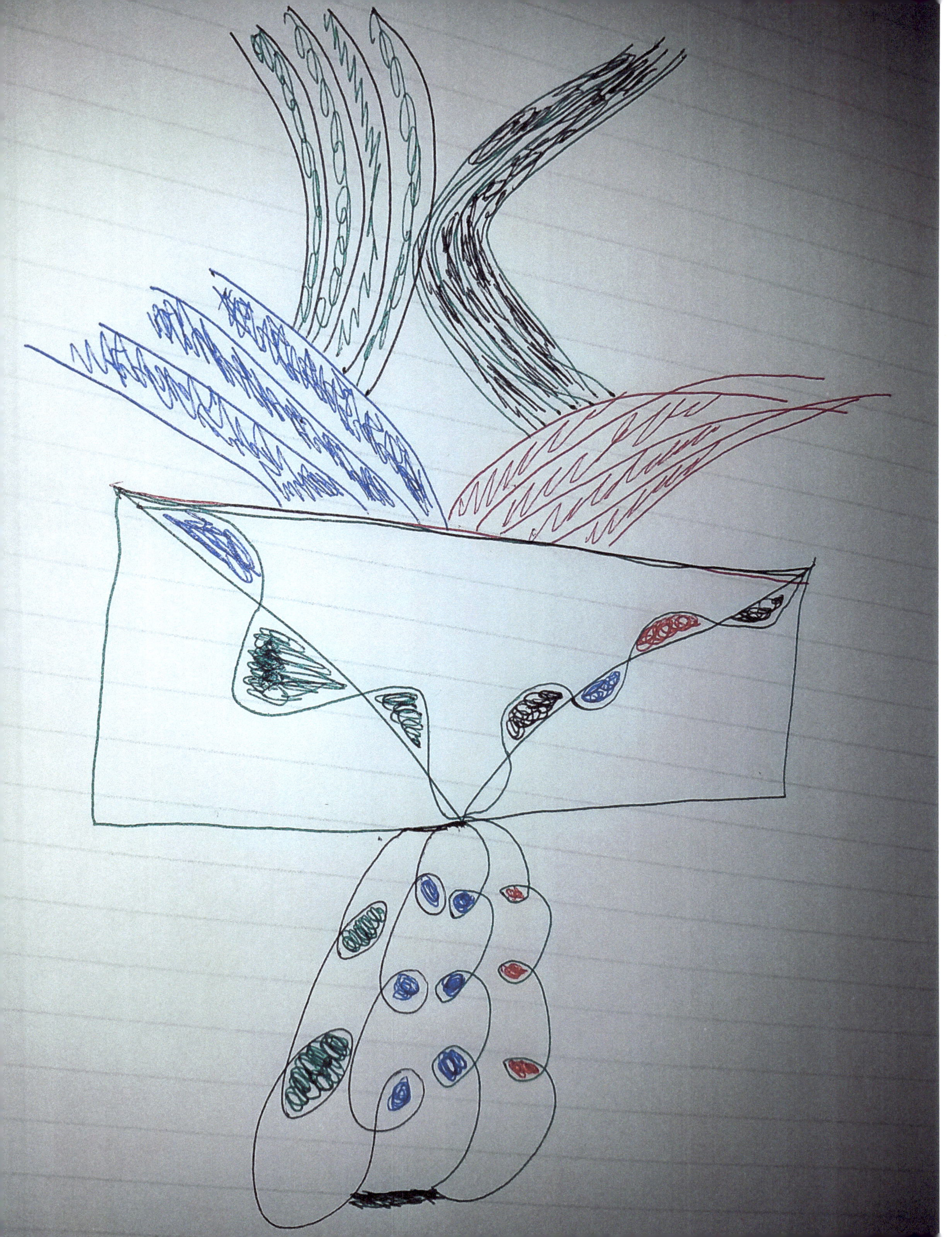

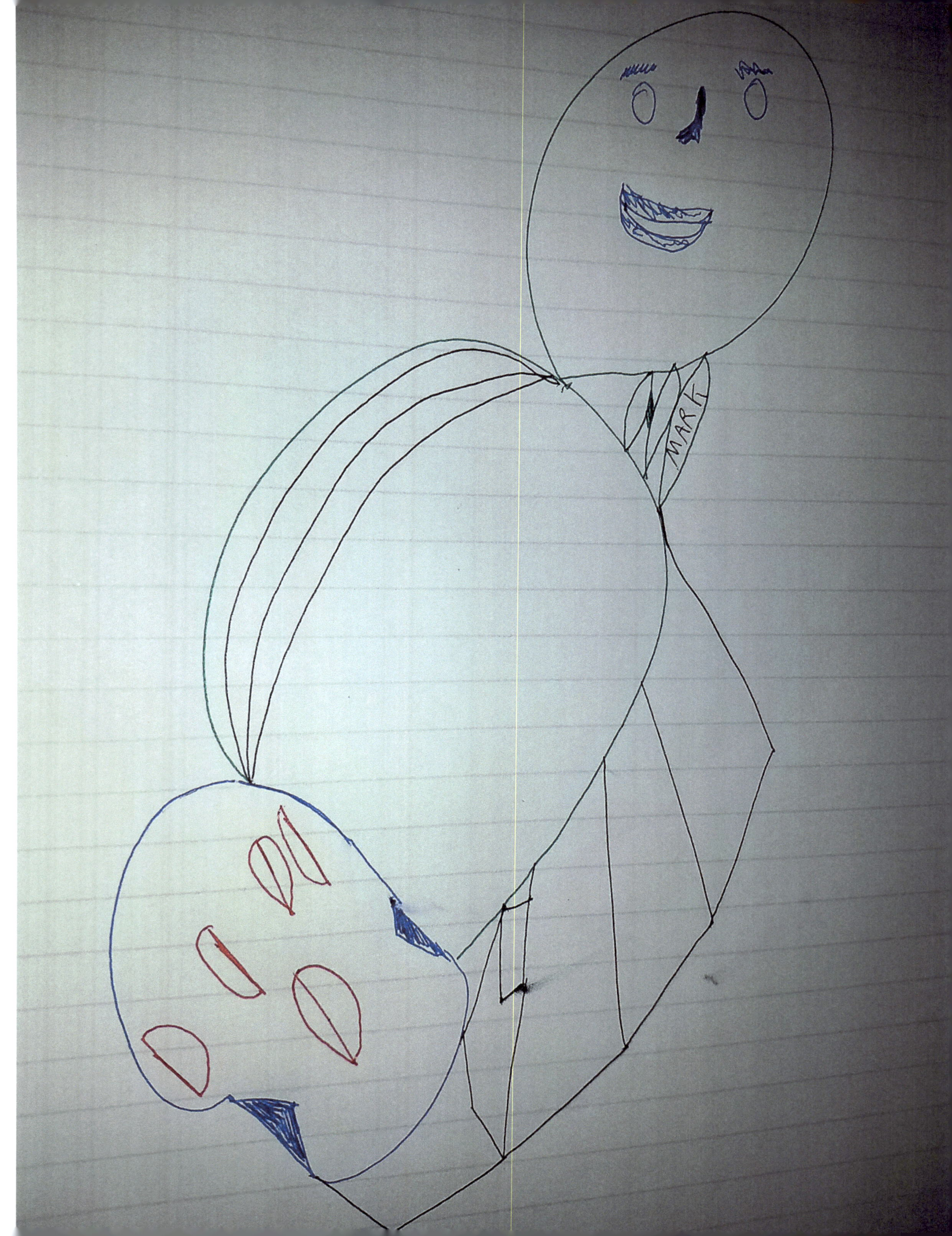
MARK

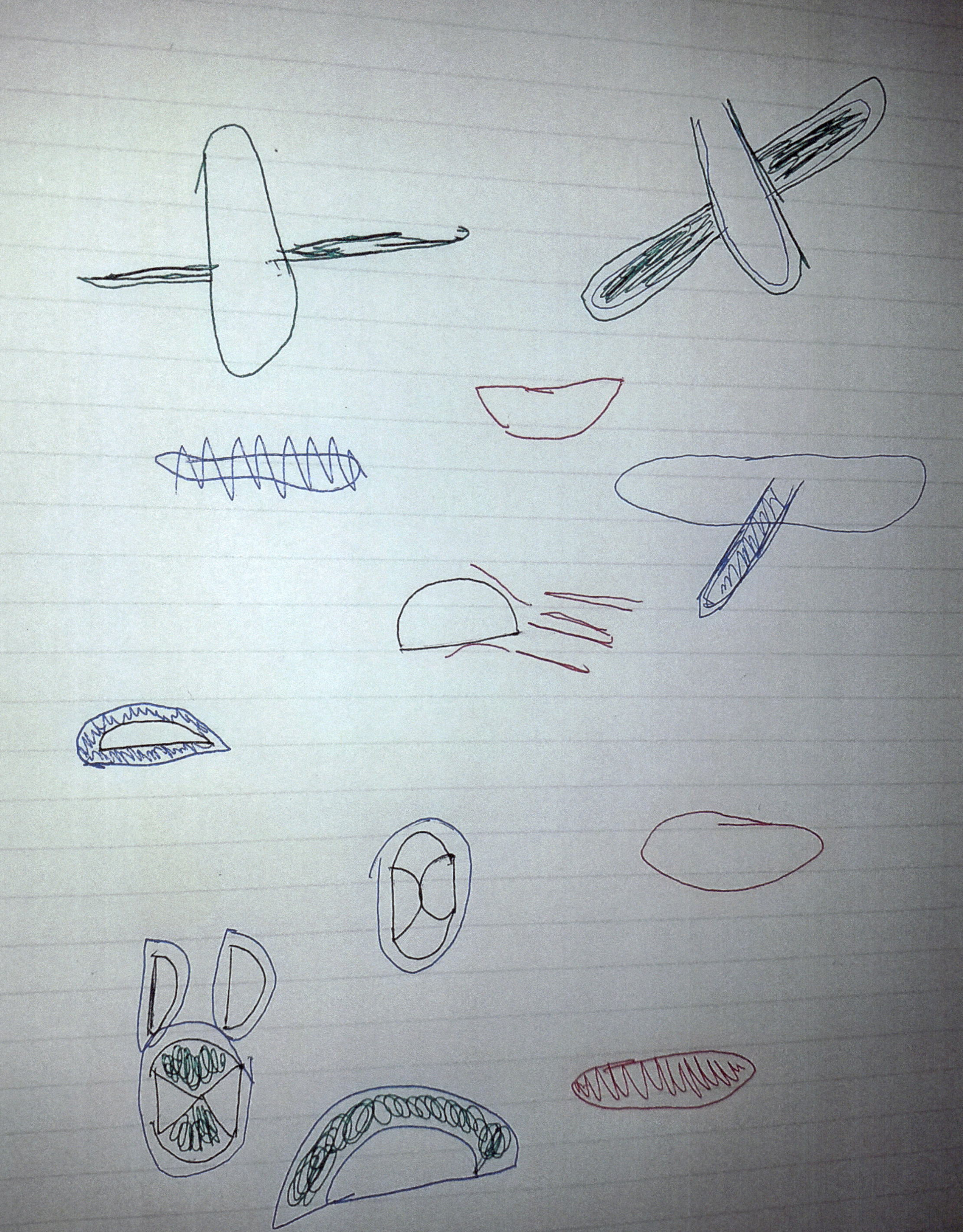

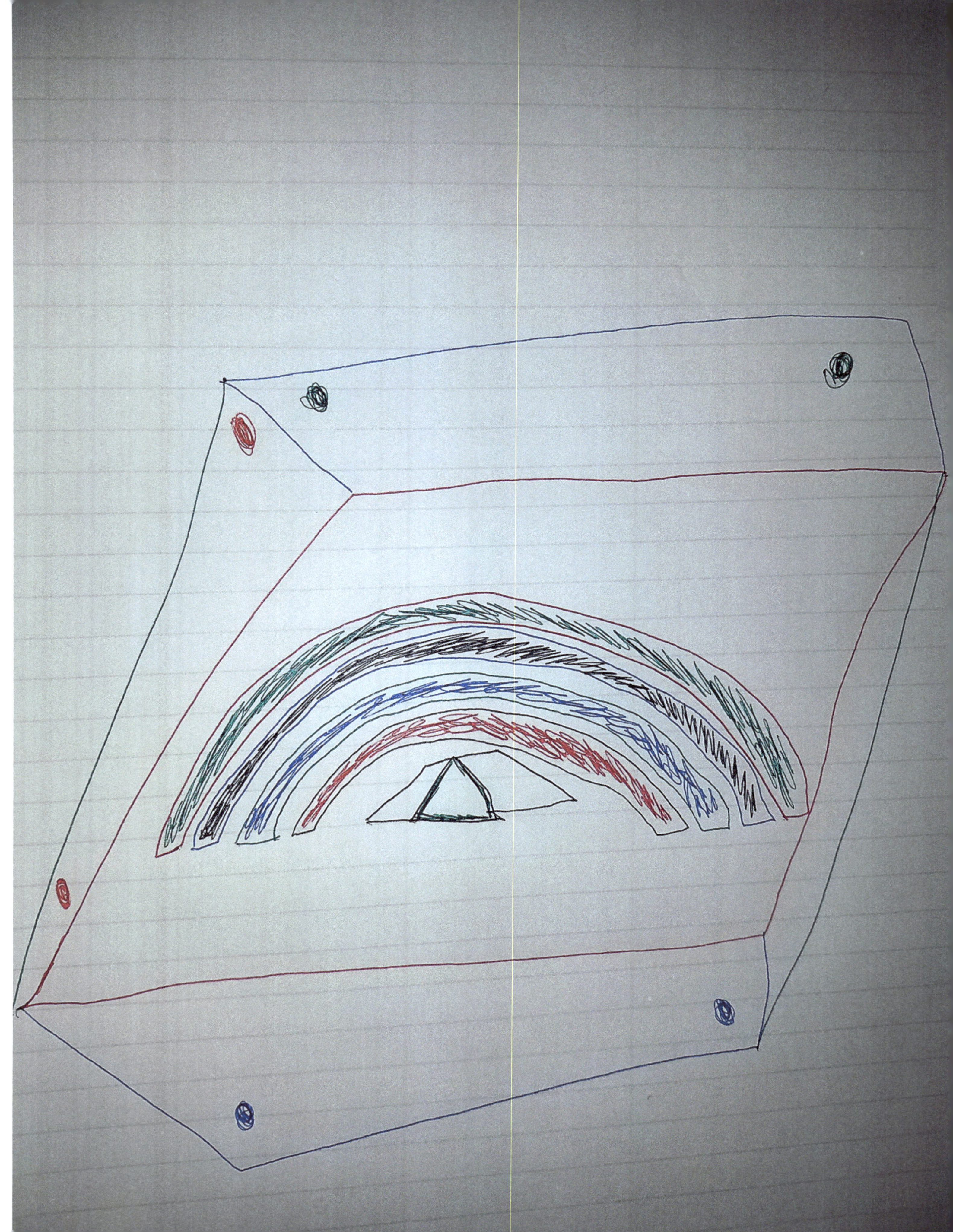

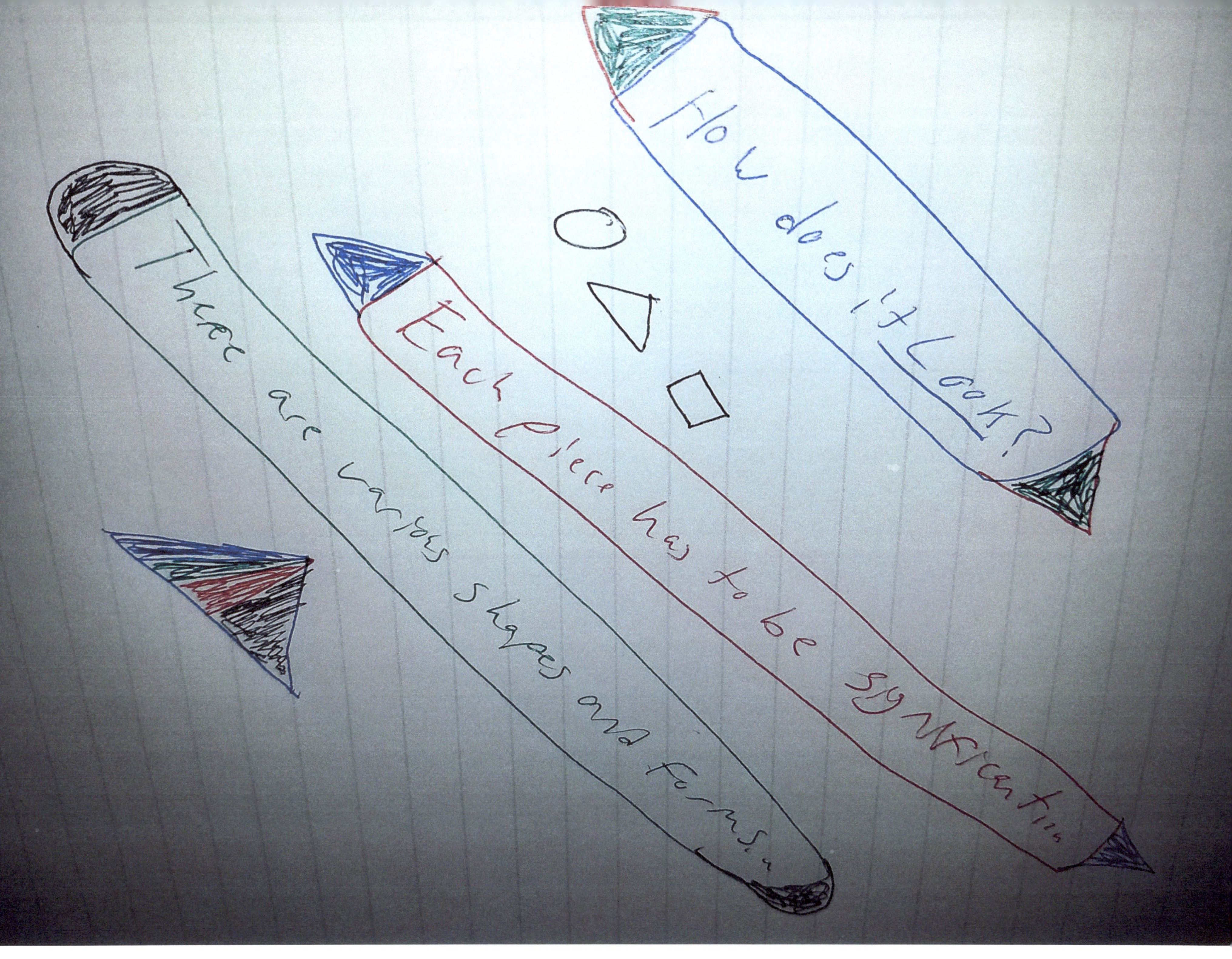

How does it Look?
Each piece has to be significant...
There are various shapes and forms...

I Just figured out that I Am a
Medical experiment

I mean, the group home I am in is a
whole 20 feet away from a
Medical hospital

Obviously whats been happening is
that Doctors and Neuroscientists in
the hospital have been manipulating
my neurology and biology for the past
2 years since I have been here

I think there was even stuff in me
for the past decade that they have
the stupid state of Massachussetts
has been manipulating

Green

well, this was my
first coloring
, its a small
drawing
however the
marker/pen
seems to be
extremely BRIGHT

Teal

Marye Bettinelli

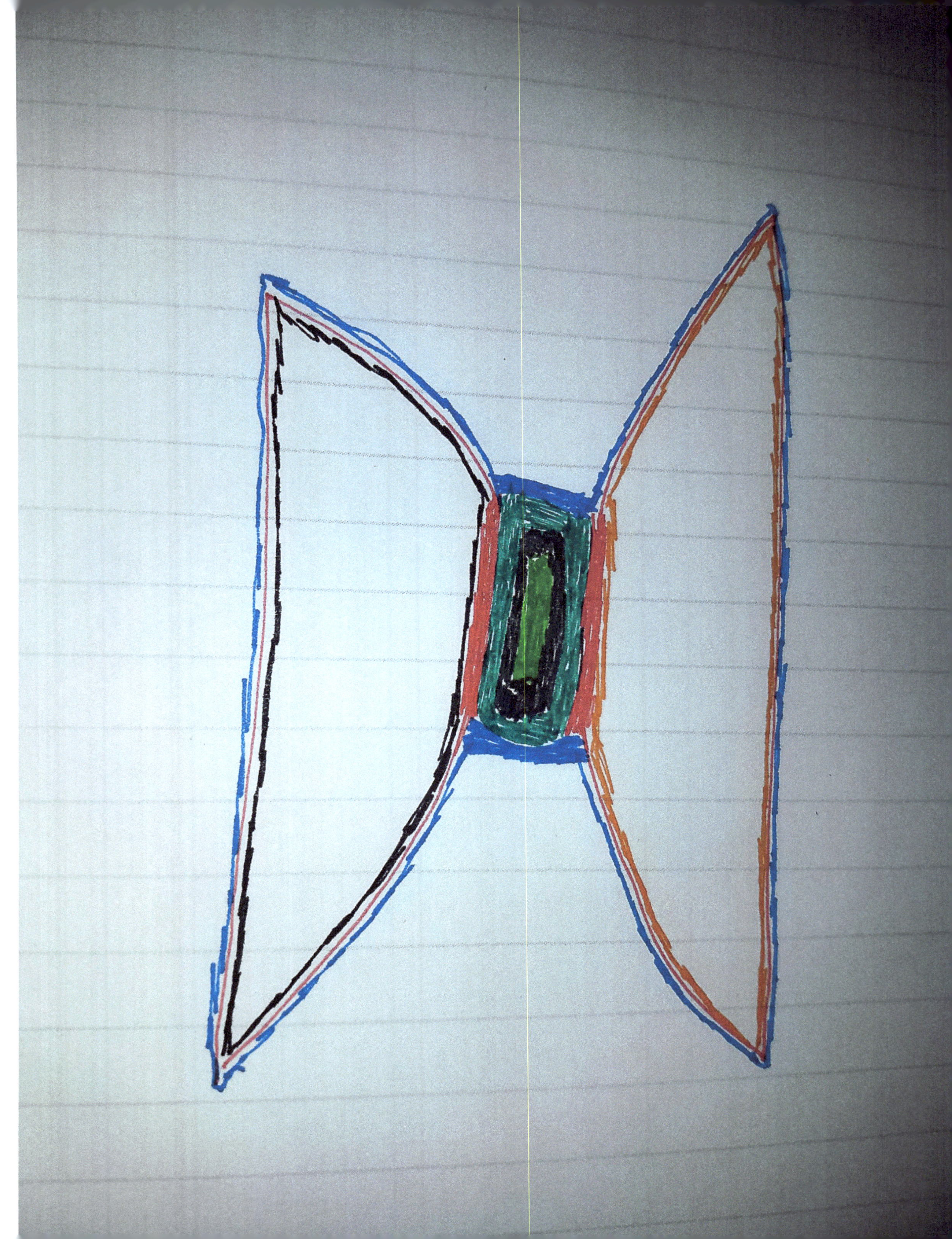

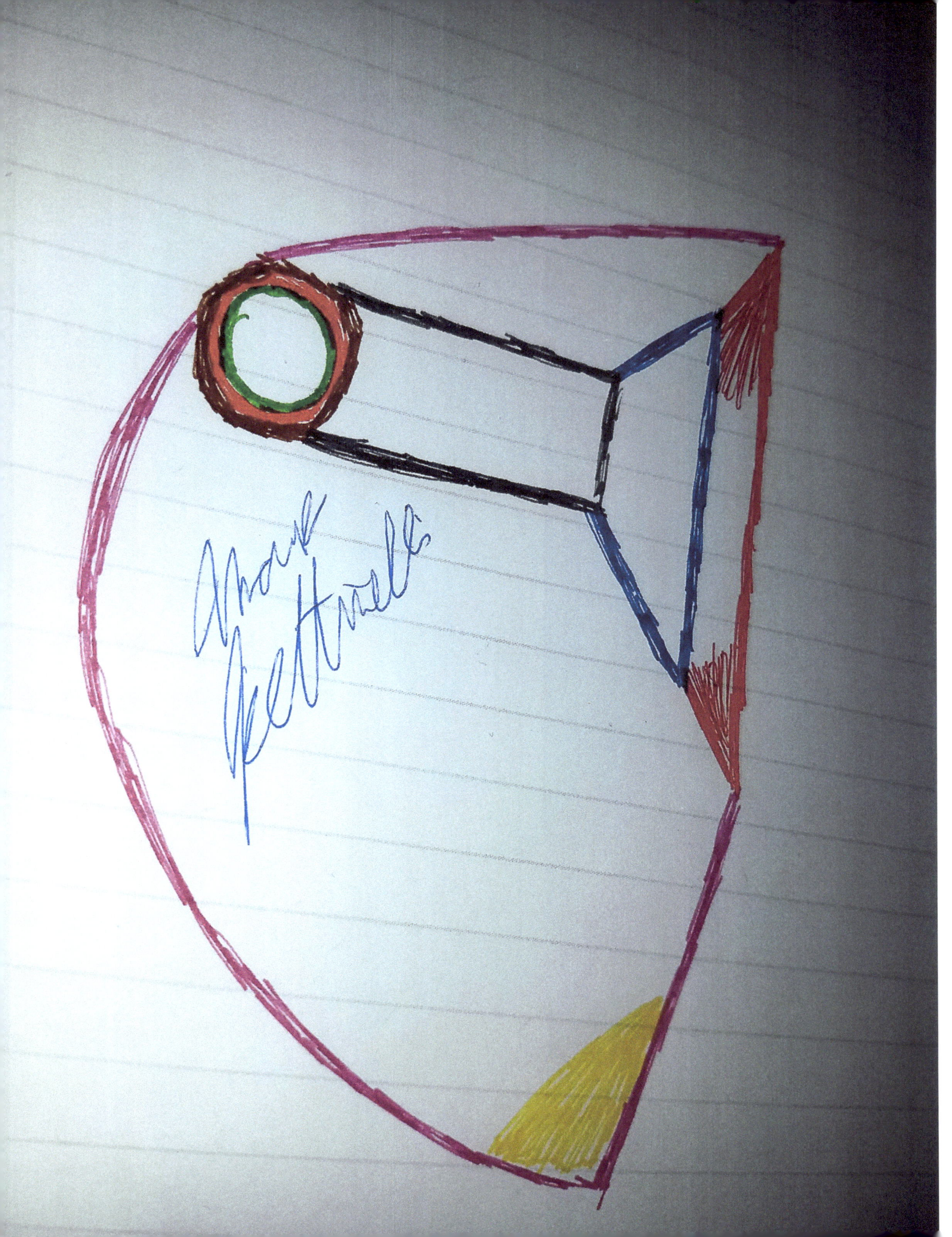

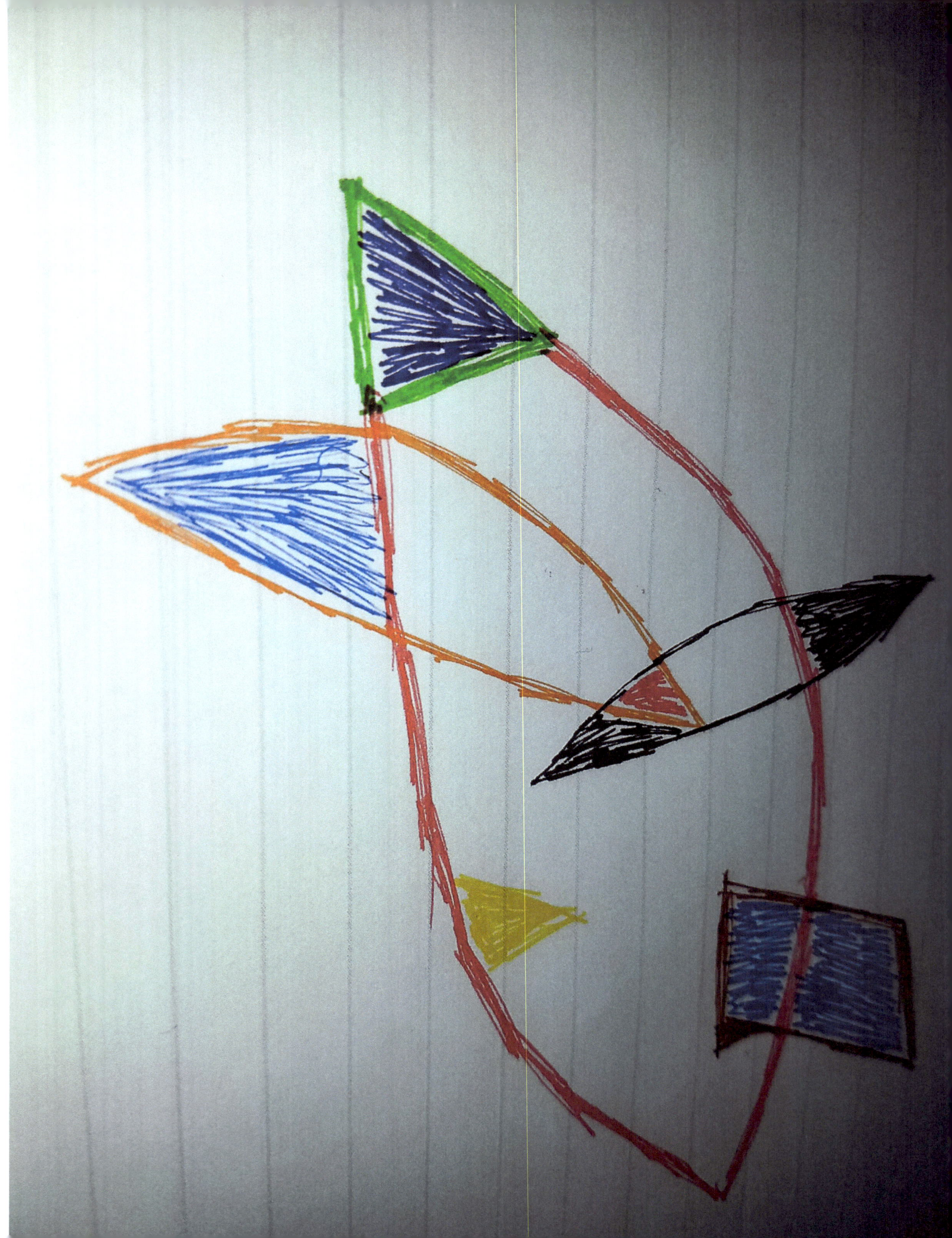

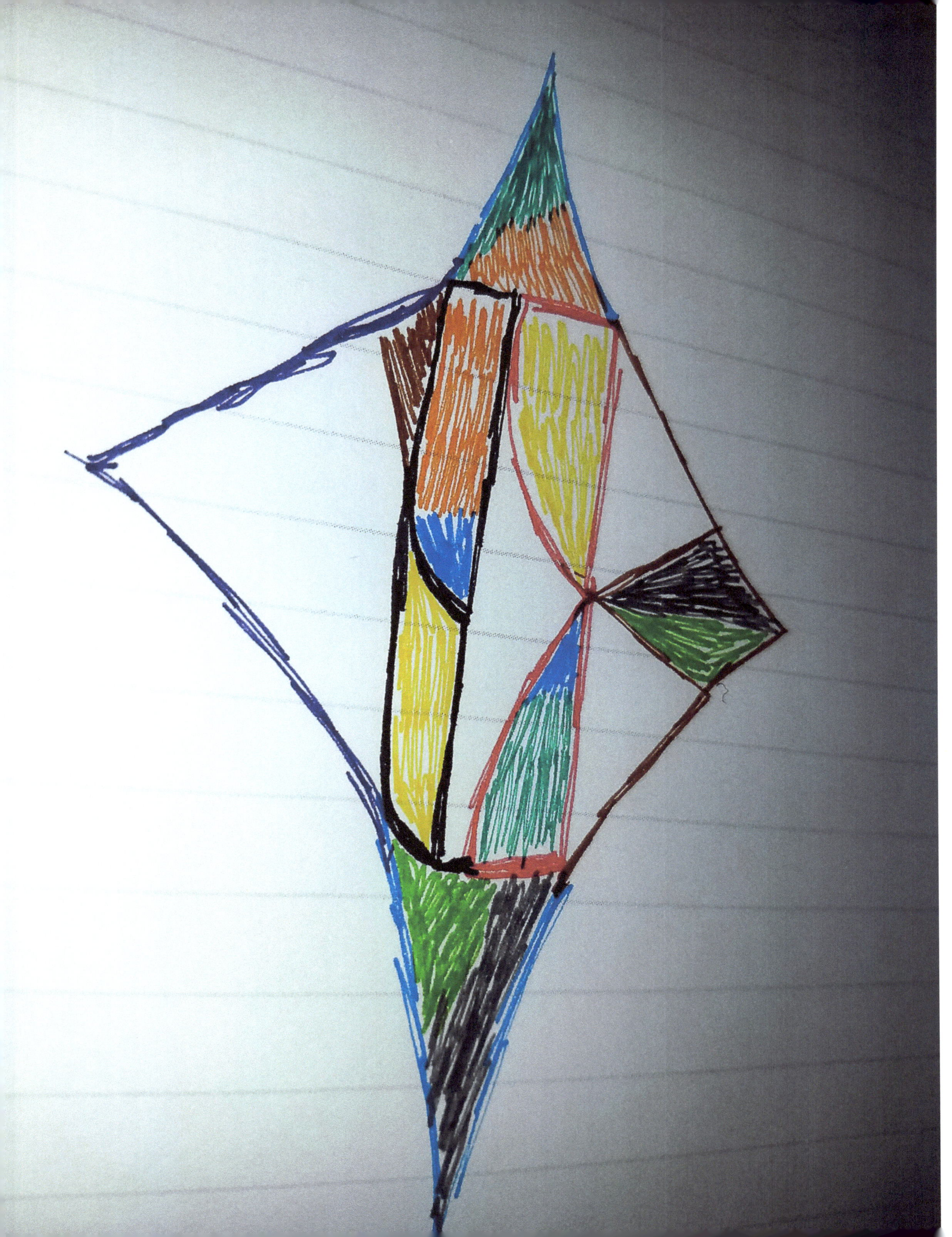

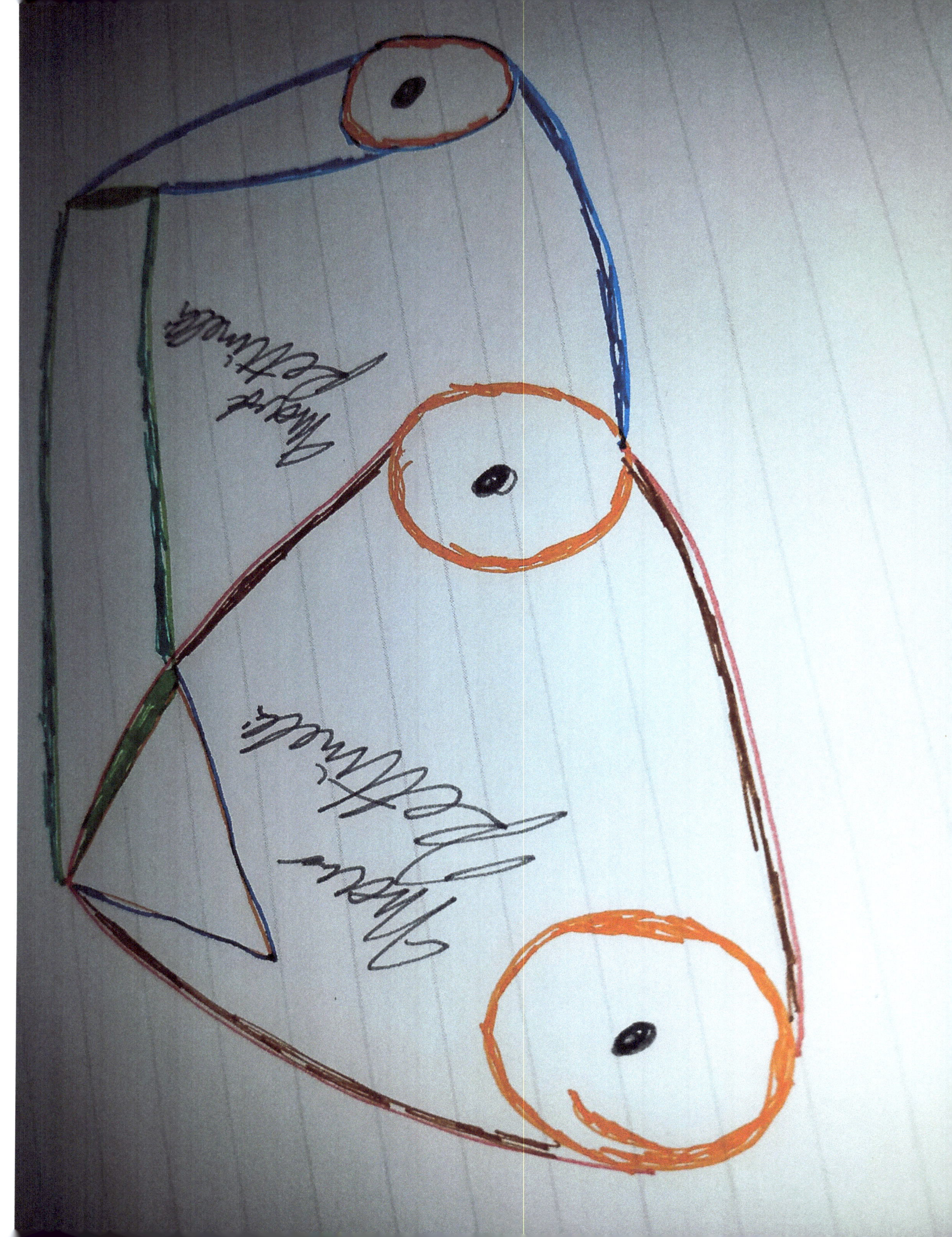

OK so, there used to be real humans,
they all died a year ago and over the
past year gravity has increased
several times. I have become
a Robot, through extreme physical pain
nanorobots in my body and mind have
turned me into a robot, a humanoid Robot
I am not too upset because I am now
immortal because I have a Robot body

and once they start making humans
in <u>INCUBATION CHAMBERS</u>

I will be capable of having fun with

the best of them

Mark Rosen Pettinelli

My name is Mark Rosen Pettinelli
My ~~middle~~ ~~name~~ online handle
that I use is Xicomik

I now am extremely powerful, so
I only need to do what my mind
needs to stay alive.

That isn't to very much because
I created the universe at the
beginning of time — so I am
powerful.

The oldest person is a *new* person,
I am from the beginning of time

Technology has advanced considerable
and the AI — Artificial Intelligence
that controls earth now knows that
it has to keep me alive or the
universe will end.

So I can easily [illegible] out of hiding and
making demands, they have no option
but to give me super hot lesbian
teenagers to satisfy me for
eternal stimulation

Mark Pettinelli

Ideas can be clear, or easy to understand
if an idea is clear then it can be simple
or easy to understand.

But what does the word 'understand' mea anyway?
when someone understands something, then
what is it that they understand, so to speak?

Humans can understand different ideas or concepts,

Ideas and concepts can be about different things,
for instance I could understand physical concepts,
i.e, a concept or Idea that is about
a concrete object.

or I could understand ideas that are about
other types of information.
Ideas could be about other people, people
that you like or Hate (dislike), or other
things that someone could think about.

OK, so this means that Humans or people
can think about different stuff.
when someone thinks about something
an idea forms in their head.

Mark Pettinelli

Categorization Categorize

Means to organize different topics, ideas or objects in a certain fashion

For instance a tree structure could be used — the word is Categorize or Categorization

Mark Pettinelli

Mark Pettinelli

Different TOPICS

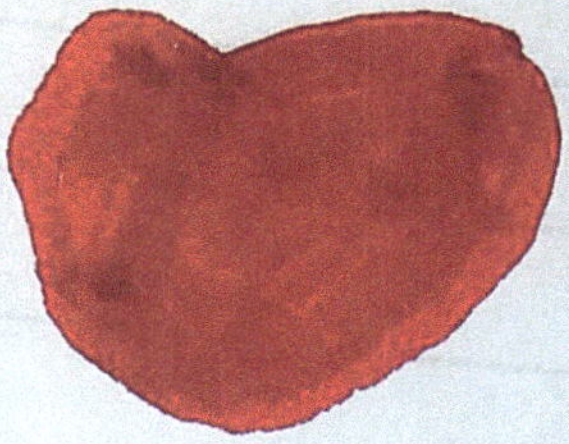

Ideas

CATEGORIES

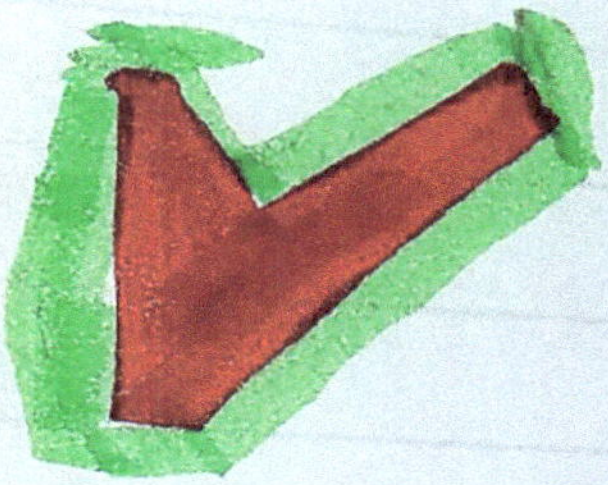

Nature

Art

Science

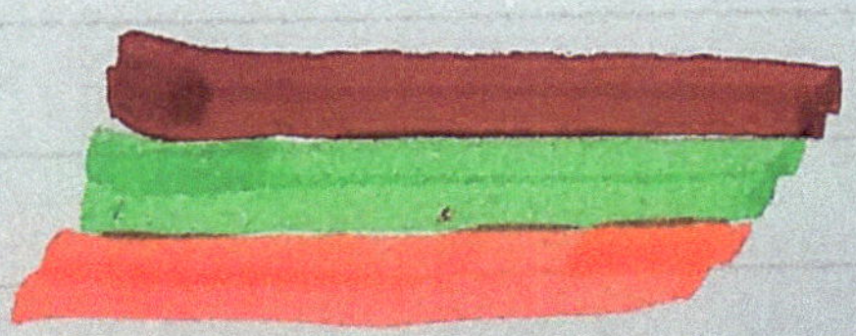

Biology

Psychology

Separate
and
Organize

Idea Categorization

Mark Pettinelli

Mark Rothblatt

Look, the Company AI,

Artificial Intelligence Completely knows that It has to Keep me alive.

OK now just calm down and breath easy. I do excellent work work. I make plans of cash money.

I dont Know about the backup thing of the universe ending though.

Martine Rothblatt

Mark Pettinella

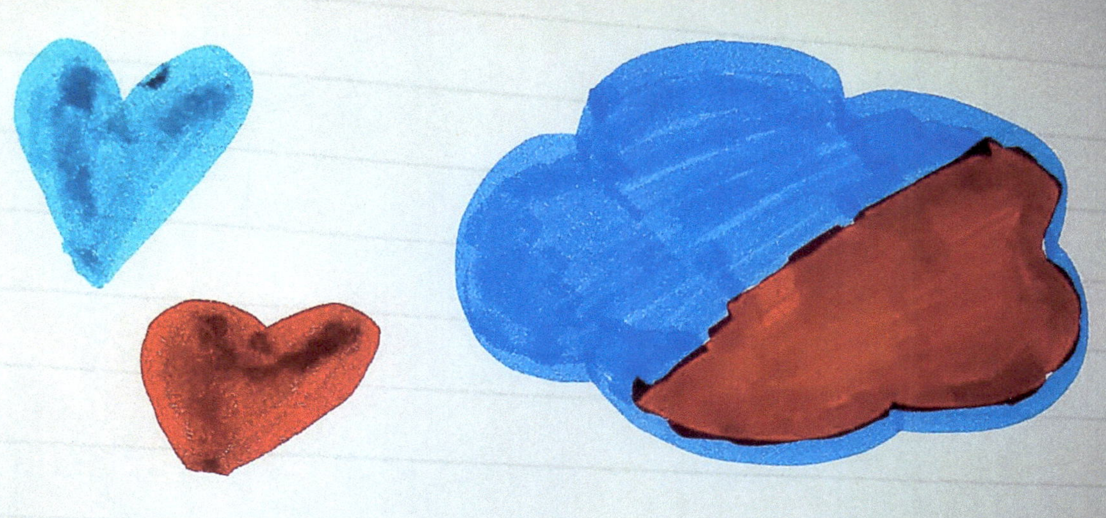

Then think about
its concept

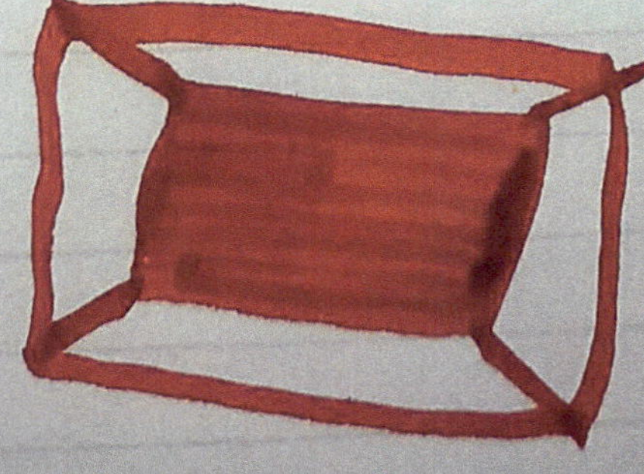

so it Makes
SENSE...

Mark Pettinella

IDEAS

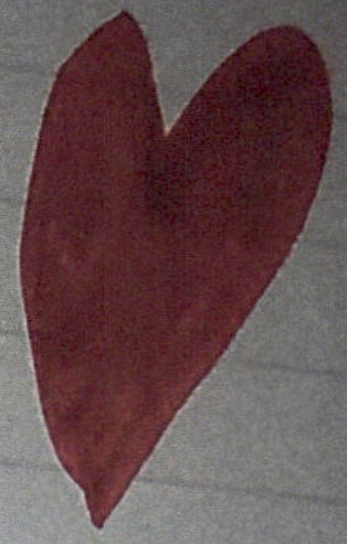

CONCEPTS

CATEGORIES

YOU CAN SEPARAT

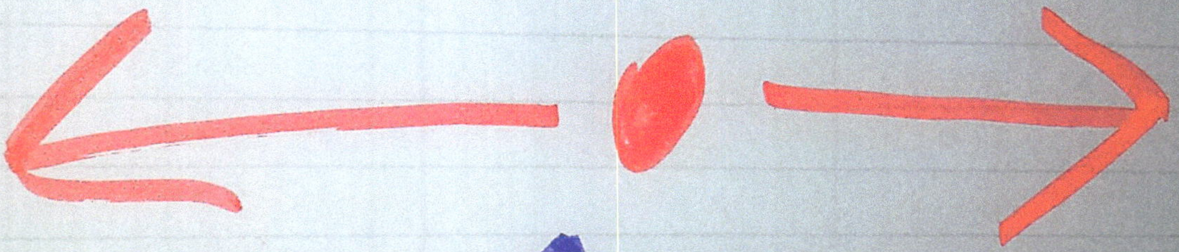

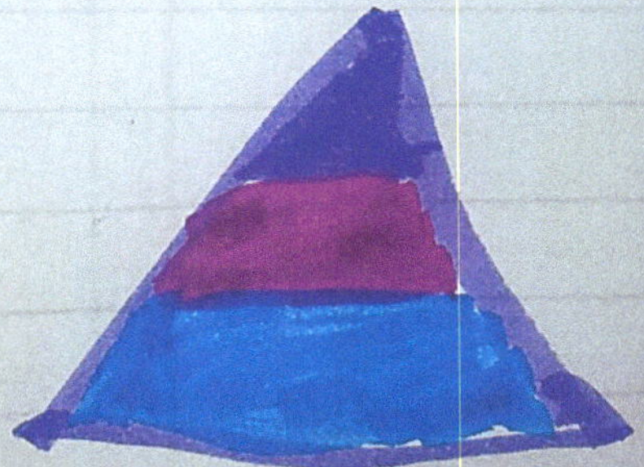

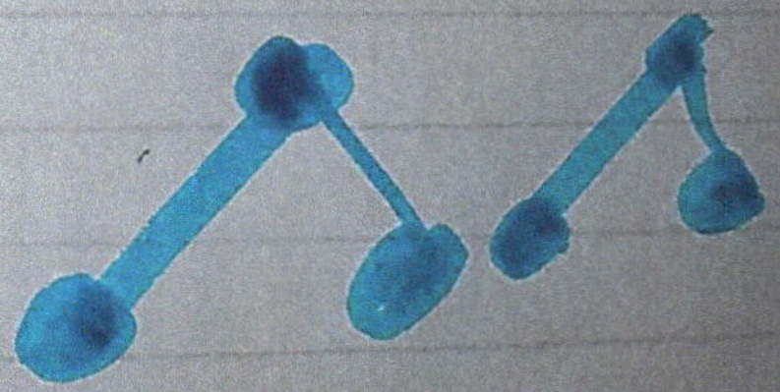

CATEGORIZE

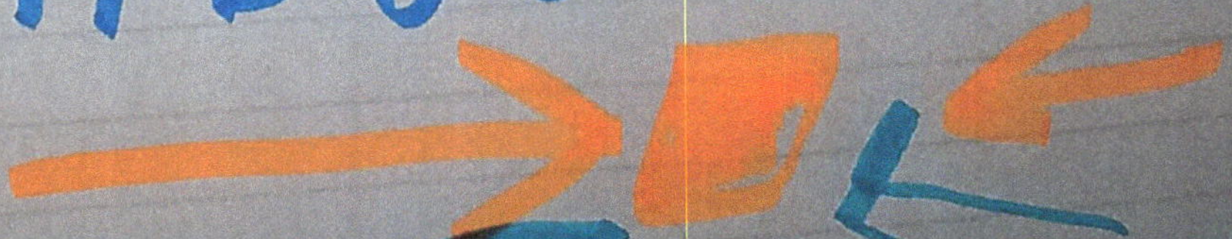

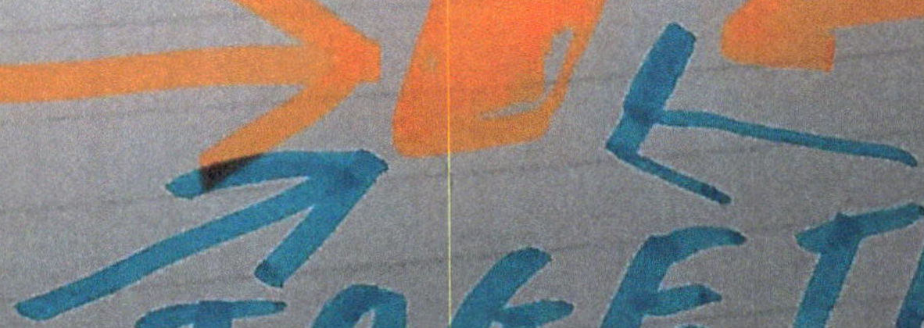

PUT TOGETHER

You KNOW THAT I LOVE YOU

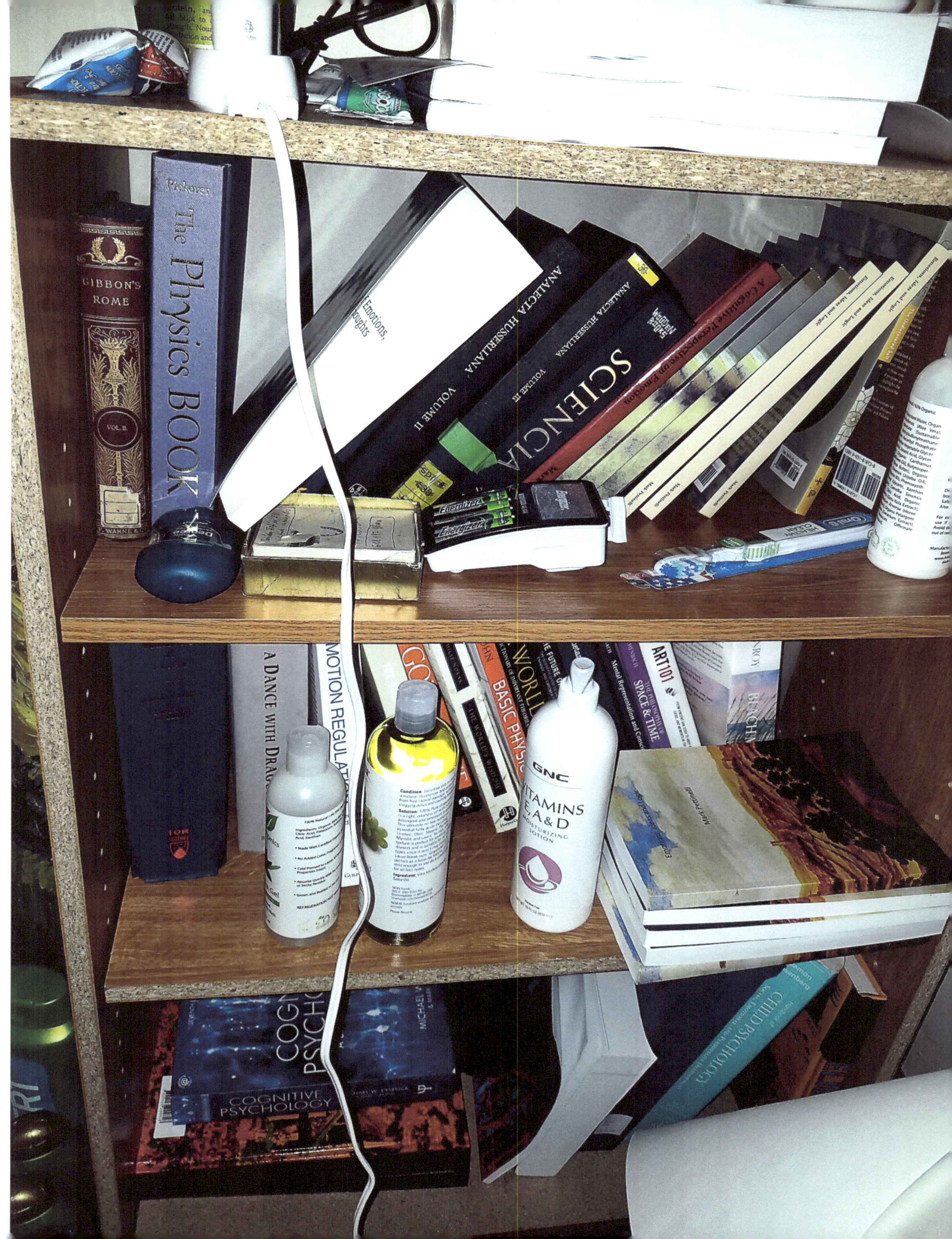

So I could write out my article multiple times to communicate more/ different information.

What is science or communication? Science is important because it is basically a rigorous or thorough understanding. What could someone achieve a thorough understanding of? If ya think about it, if something needs to be communicated then you need to first understand it.

First something is thought about, then it is thought about more deeply and then it is understood. That makes sense. If ya think about it - when someone thinks about something for the first time a type of understanding dawns on them. This understanding takes a certain period of time to figure out; however, How long does it take for someone to figure something out? That is an interesting question, In order to figure out something someone might need to make sentences in their head or think about something with words. They might also make or think about sounds to themself - think the sentence out in their head with sounds, for instance. That process could enhance how the understanding of a certain concept is thought about or understood (figured out).

That is a good question, how exactly is something figured out? It is probably more complicated than just saying the sentence of it to themselves in their heads. For instance if someone just says to themself, "well if I think about it this or that way, or if I think about this or that thing then I could understand this concept or idea better.

Sometimes people need help understanding concepts
from other people or influences in their environm
what kind of influence does other people have on hu
understanding of concepts? Understanding Concepts is importan
what kind of idea is someone trying to understand? That's a
good question, if you think about it logically then
all the ideas in life can be sorted through and organ
and it could be figured out how difficult it is to
understand each different idea.

UM SO I won't be copied - It is
Impossible to copy me because how
do I explain it. I mean looking at
me now it only looks like I weigh 280
pounds and can do push ups and walk
around, sleep and dream with normal
reflexes. I am based upon that
info you would think you could copy me

UM SO I mean, based upon looking at me
you would think you could copy me
however they dont know what an awesome athlete
I'm going to become and I'll only weigh 230 in the
future, not 280. April at the Boston Sports Club
said I could beat dave. The same I play is squash -
its kind of like racquetball except the ball is the
size of a golf ball so its alot harder

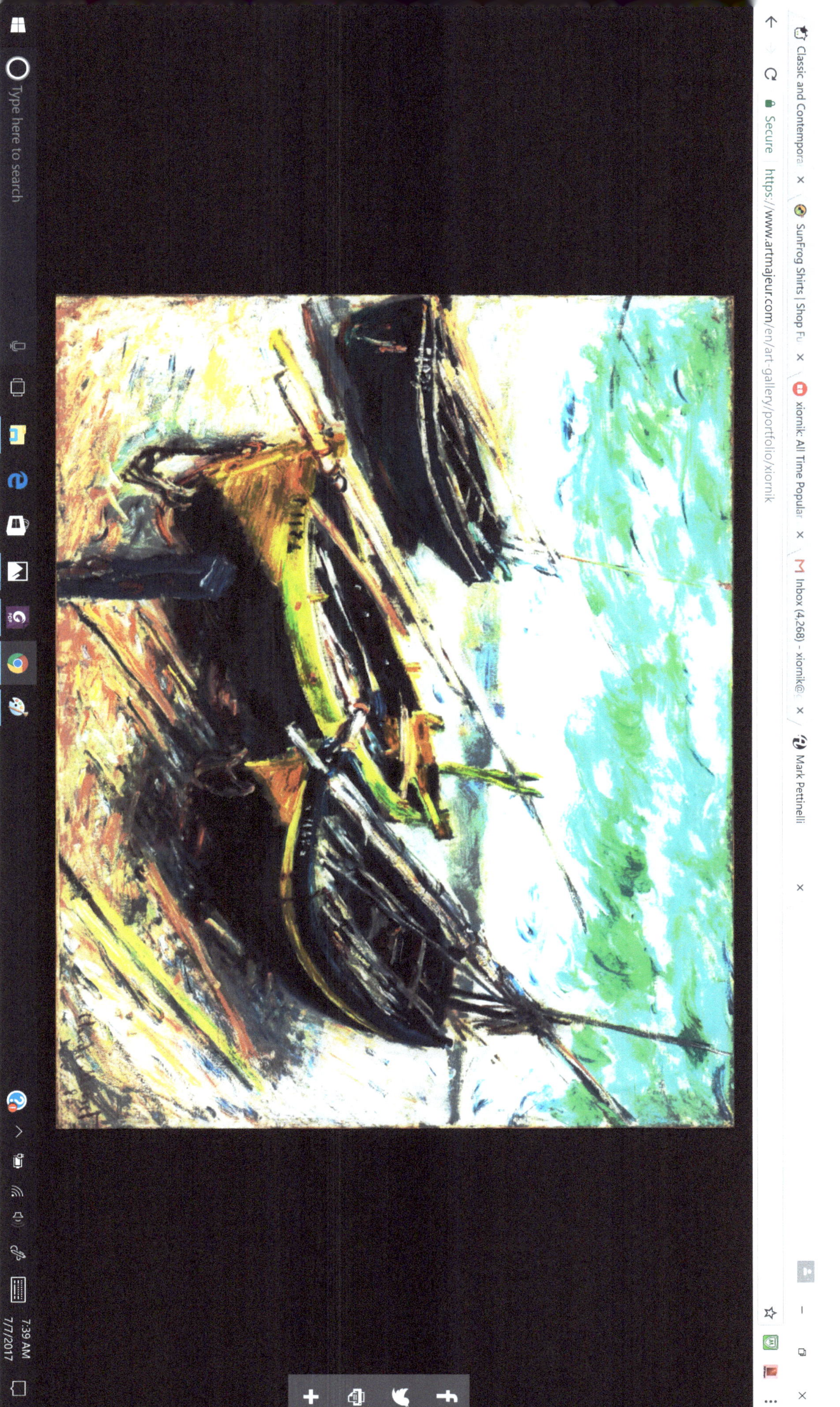

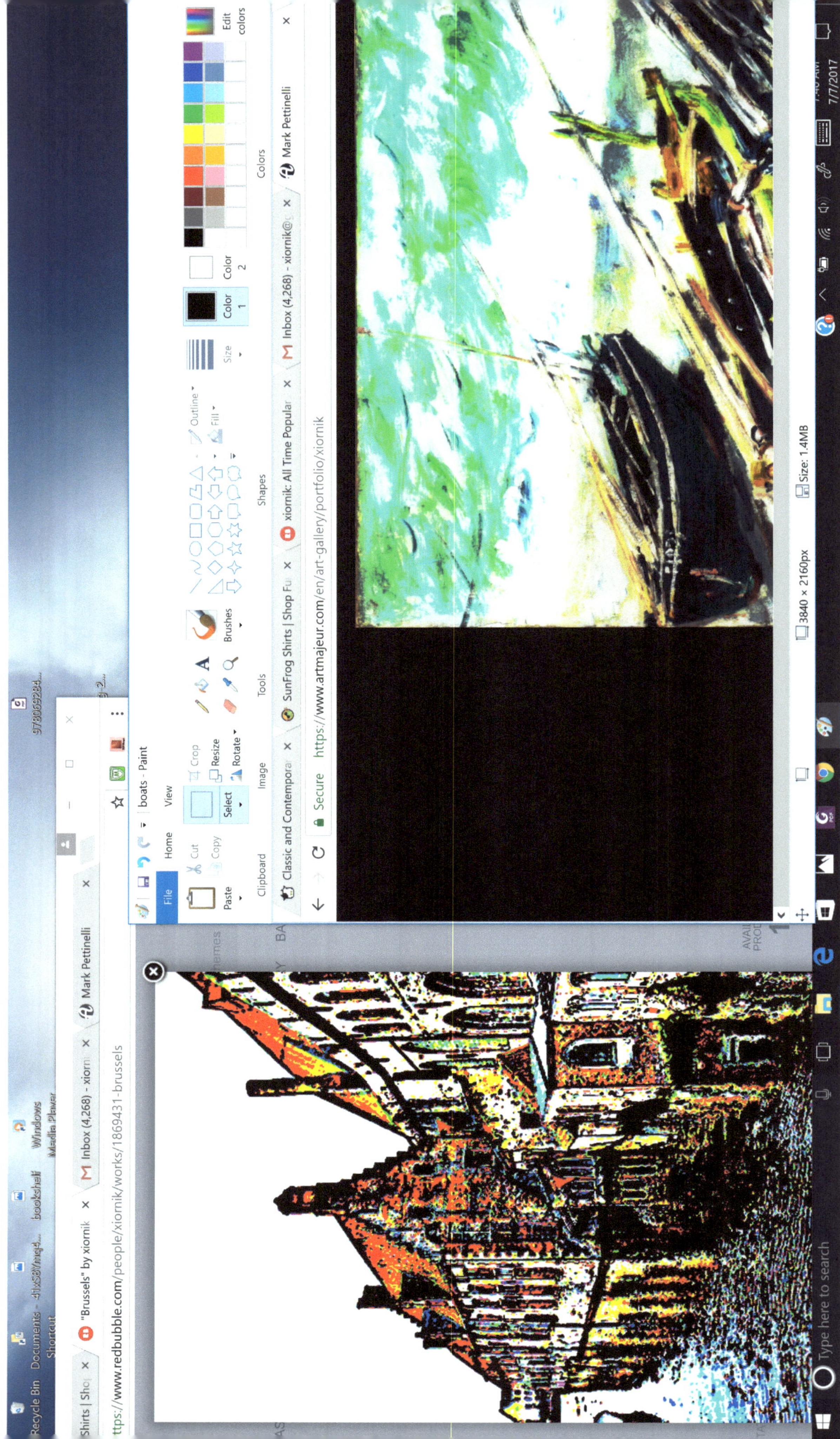

OK so, I'm responsible for a huge
amount of medical research
because I'm a nanobot, and I
get a consciousness transfer —
each time I get a transfer
my body improves because I get
transfered into a new body —
basically the consciousness component
is important, in other words —
in addition to me being a biological
robot, or as I call it, a nanobot
um so, I also listen to old music —
and those are all how do i say
this — (Rock stars?) twice
becoming fands off of me
OK so I've been next to the hospital
for 3 years and have not gotten a blowjob
from a nurse yet so...

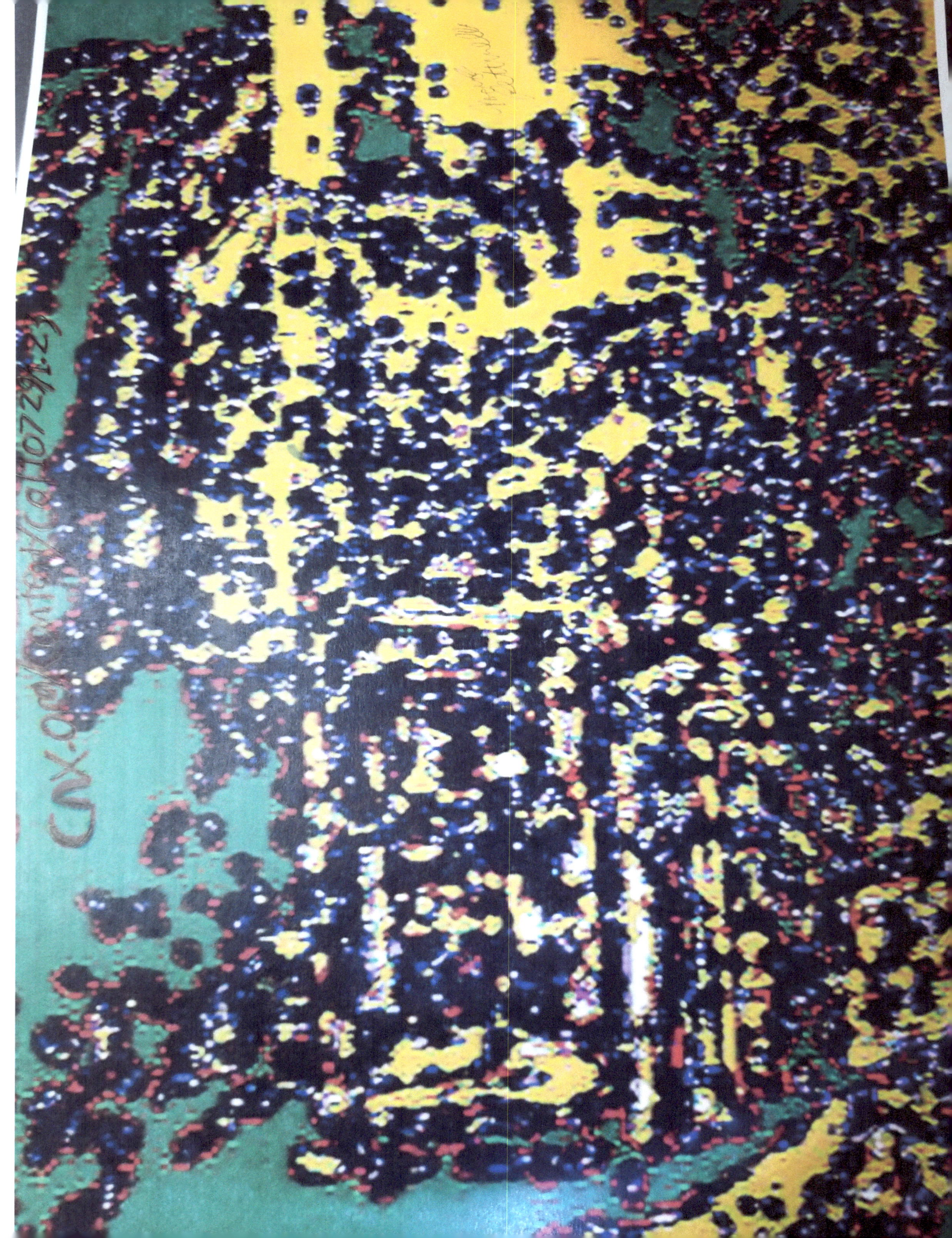

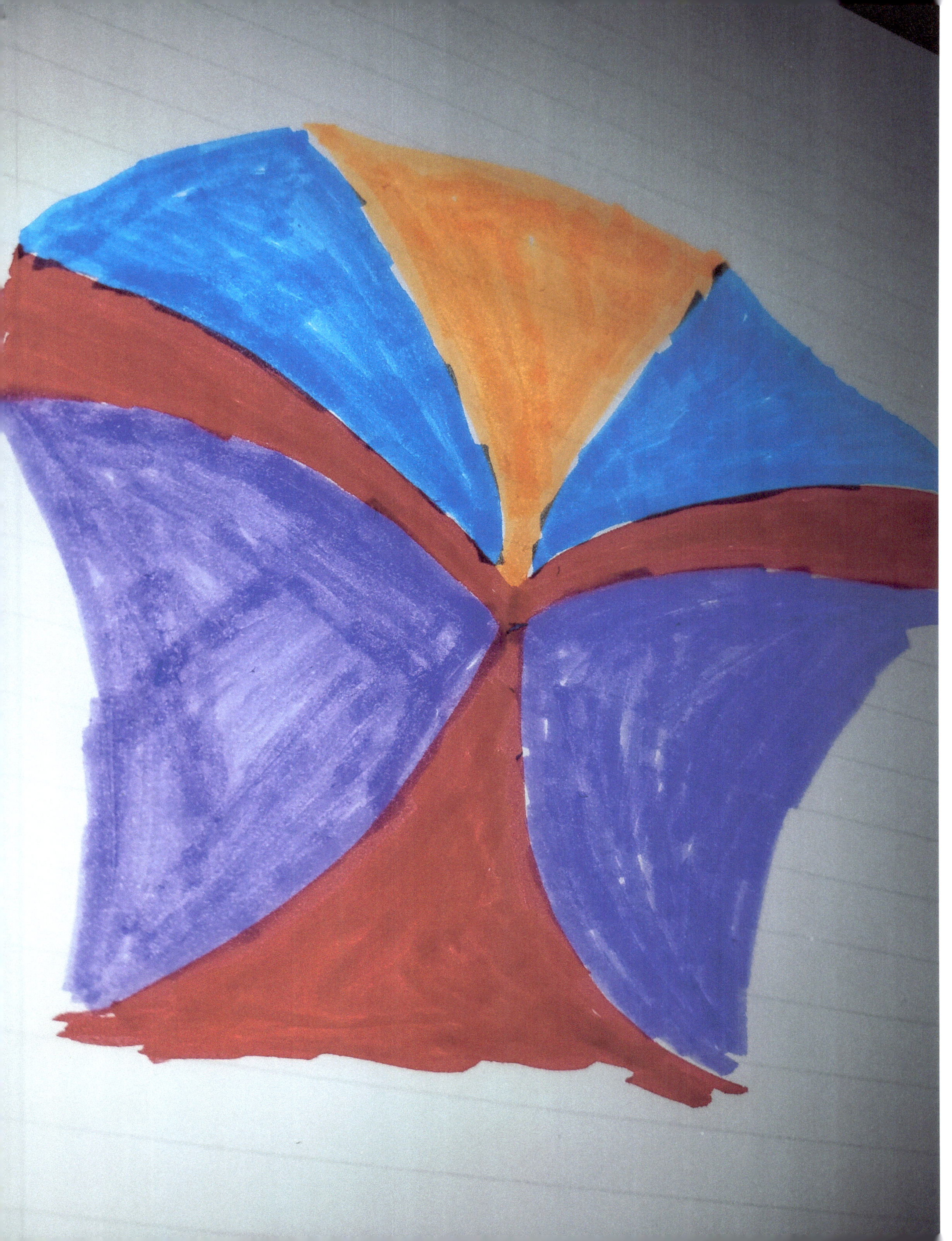

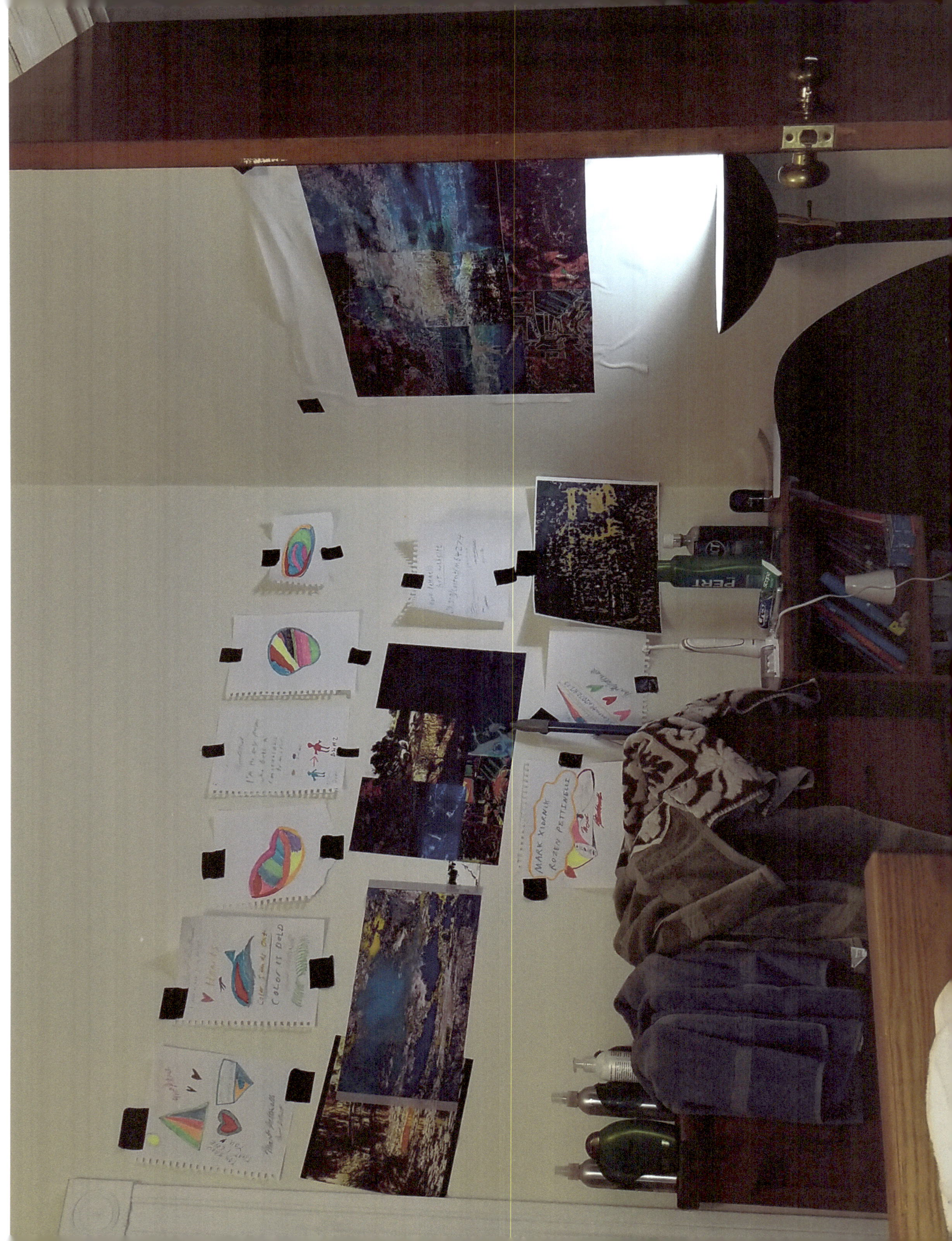

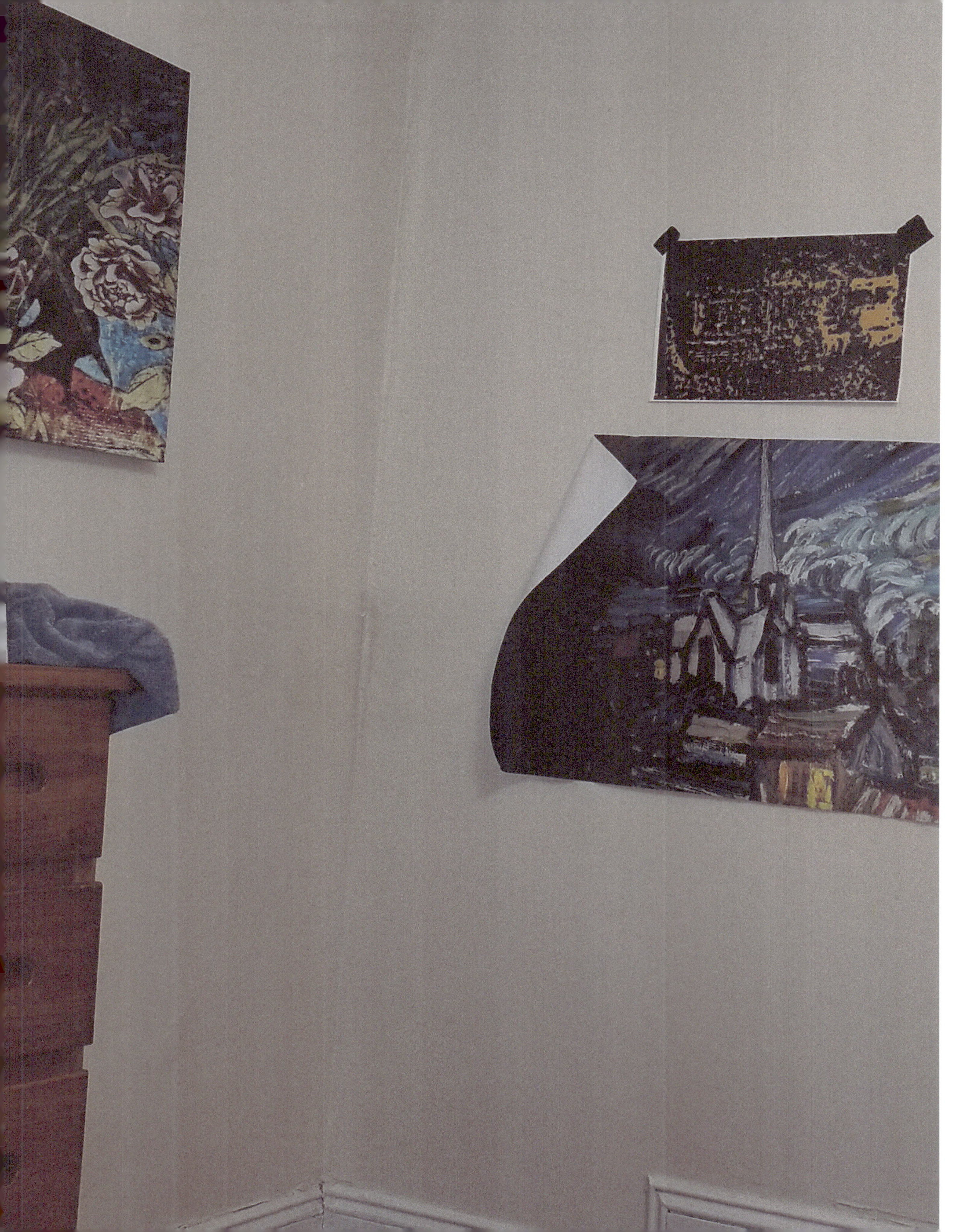

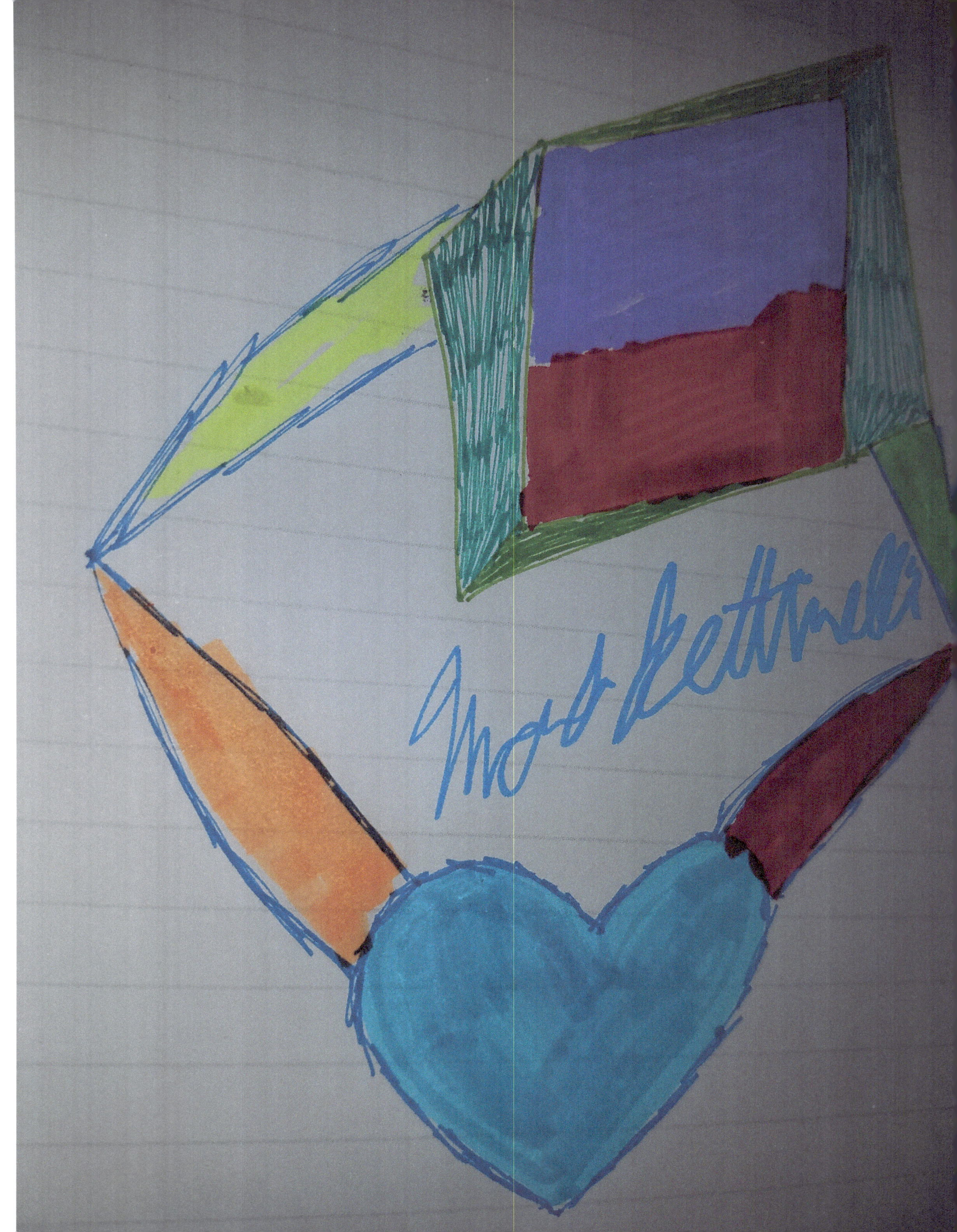

What is Important?
in life?

"Mark Rettinelli

That is a good question...

How LARGE I AM

My Consciousness Transfer

My Feelings are Important

But from where do they come?

That is another Good question

Mark Rettinelli

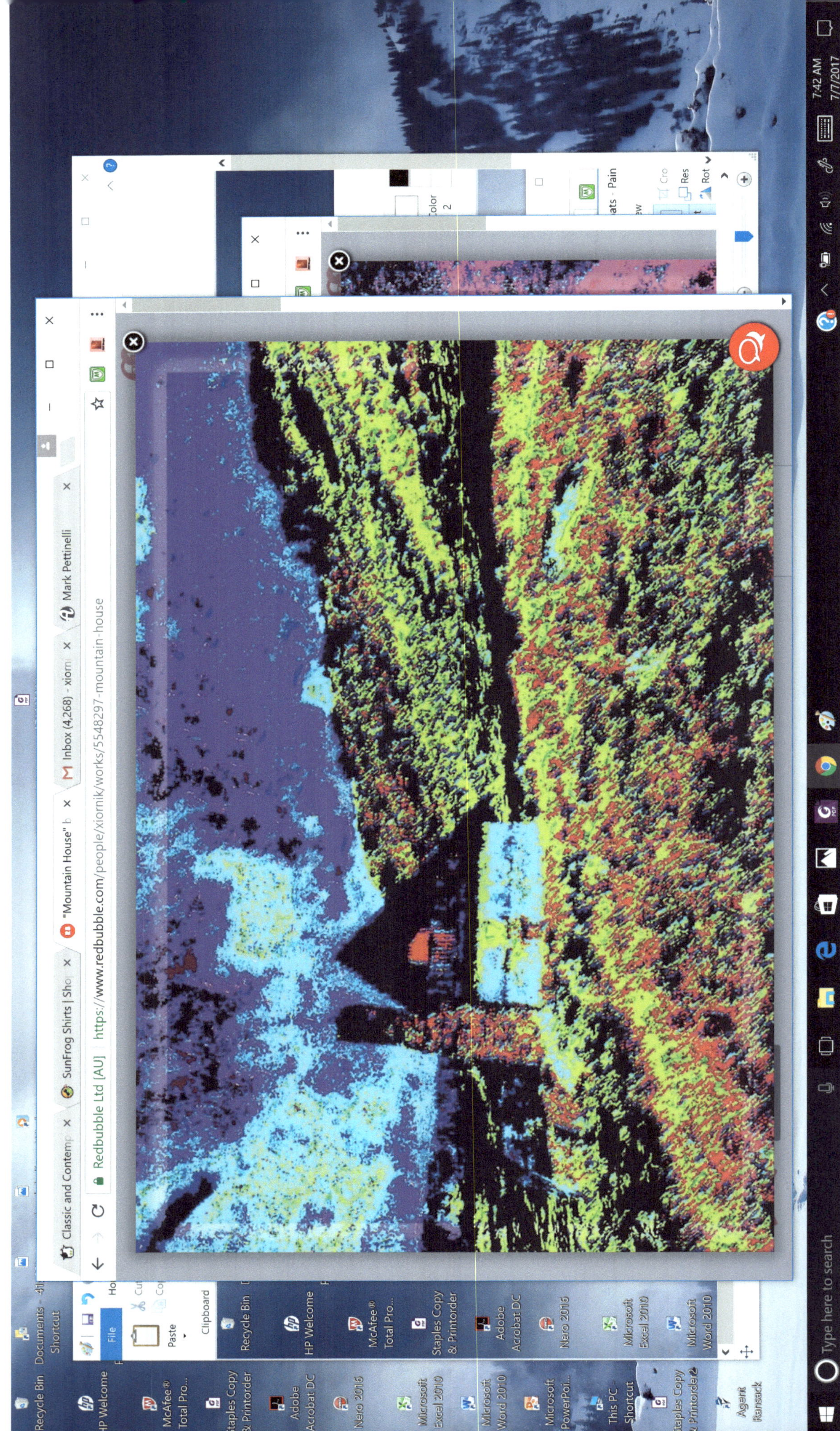

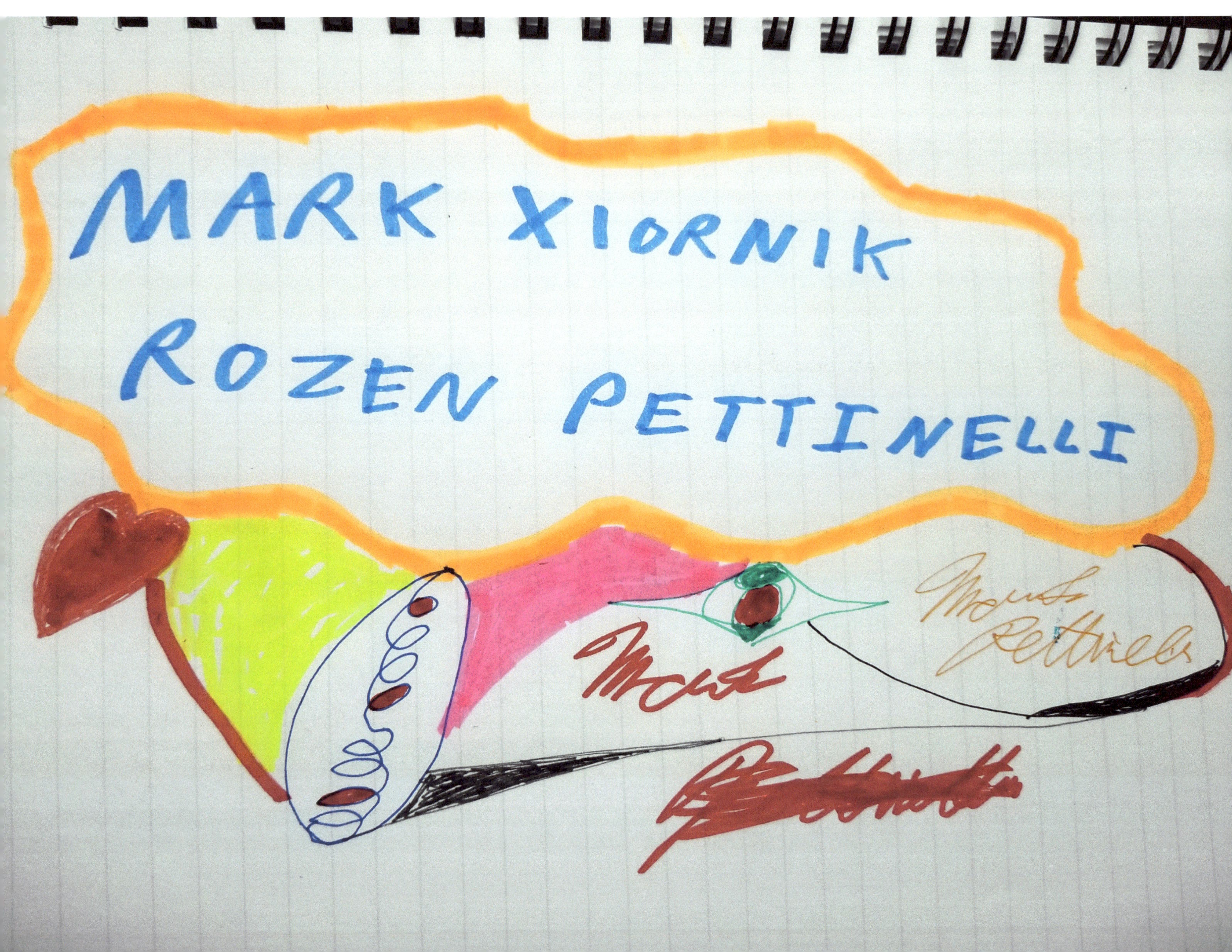

MARK XIORNIK
ROZEN PETTINELLI

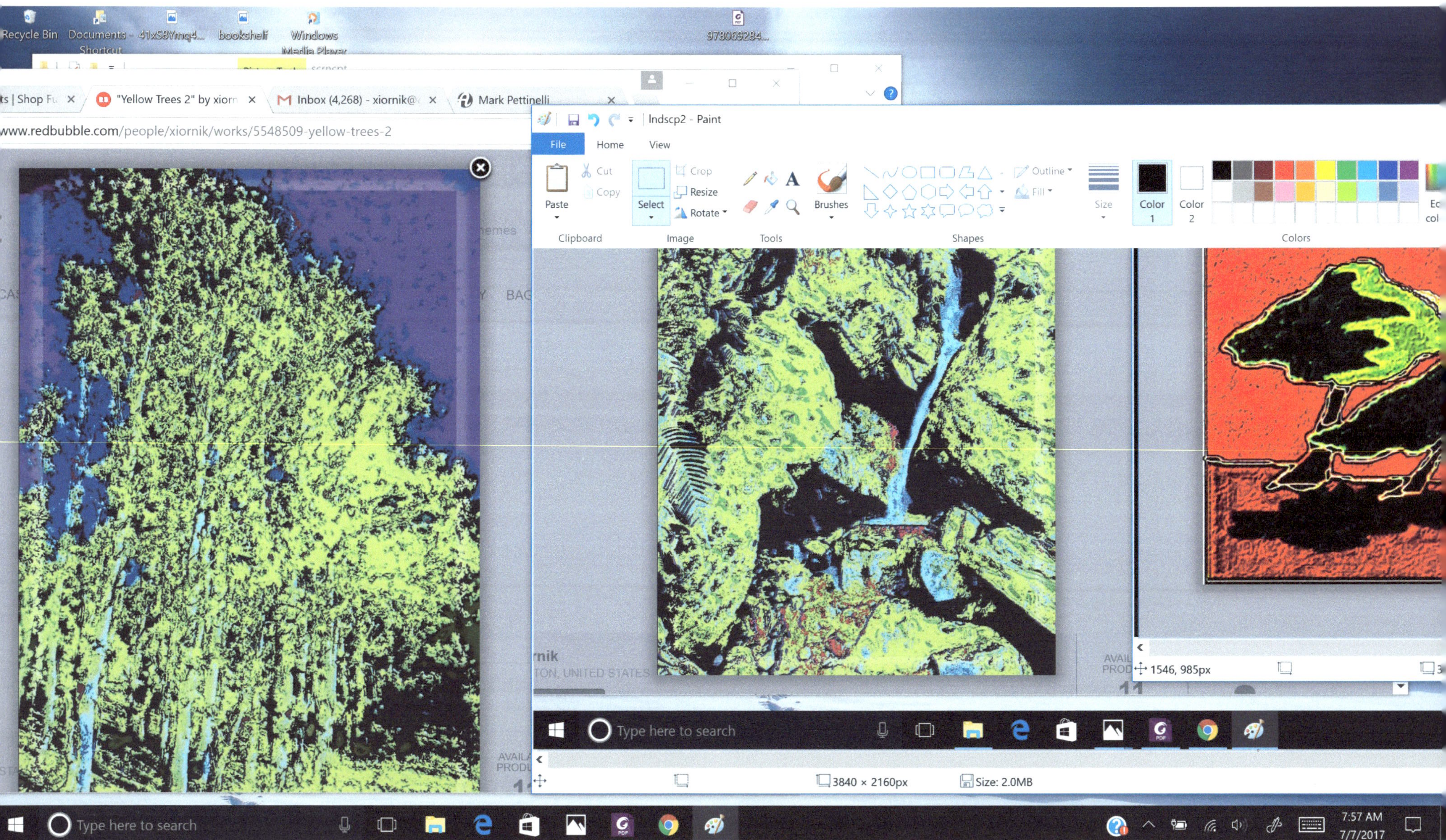
www.redbubble.com/people/xiornik/works/5548509-yellow-trees-2
Indscp2 - Paint
File
Home
View
Paste
Clipboard
Image
Tools
Shapes
Size
Color 1
Color 2
Color
3840 × 2160px
Size: 2.0MB
Type here to search
7:57 AM
7/7/2017

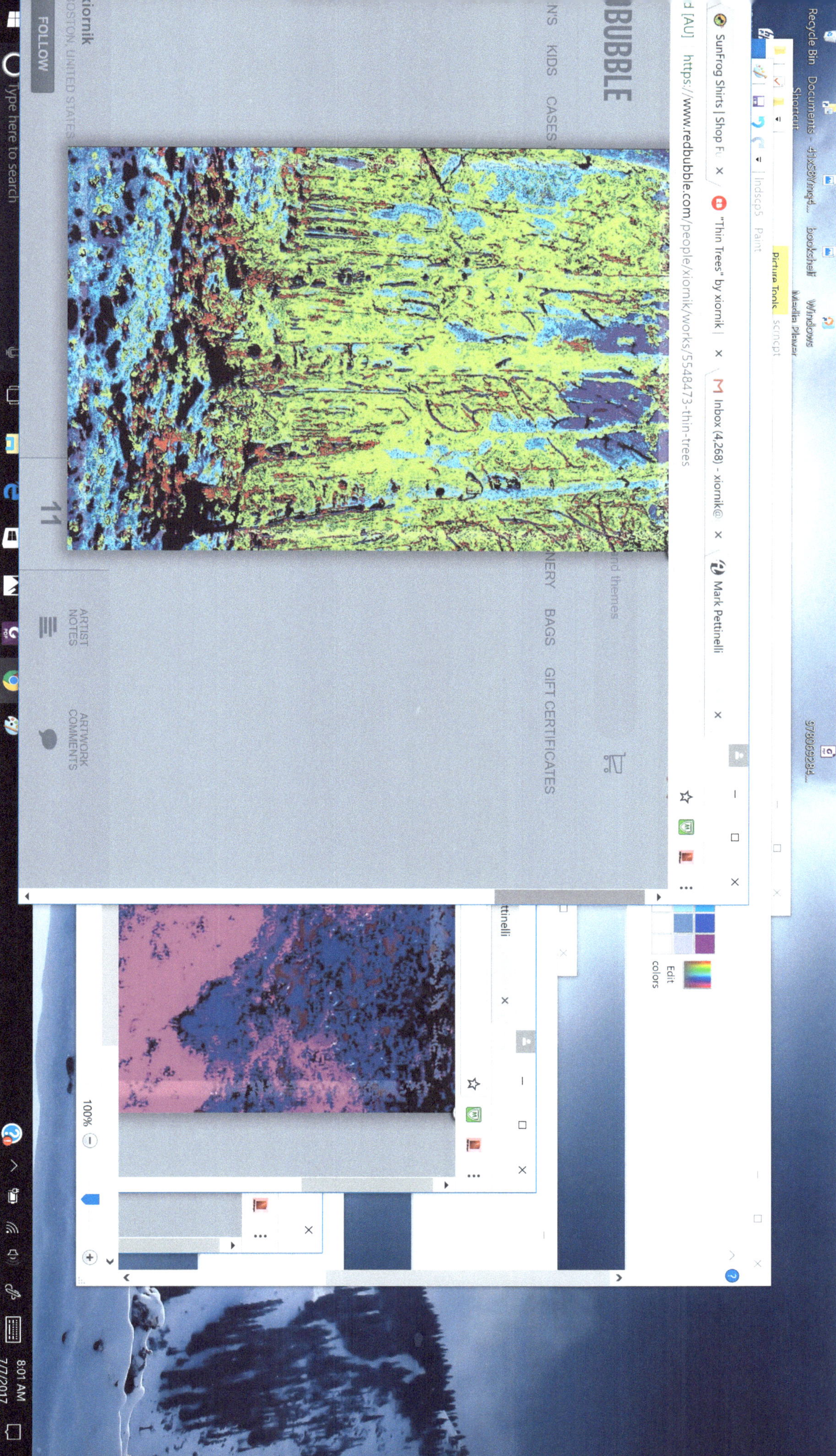

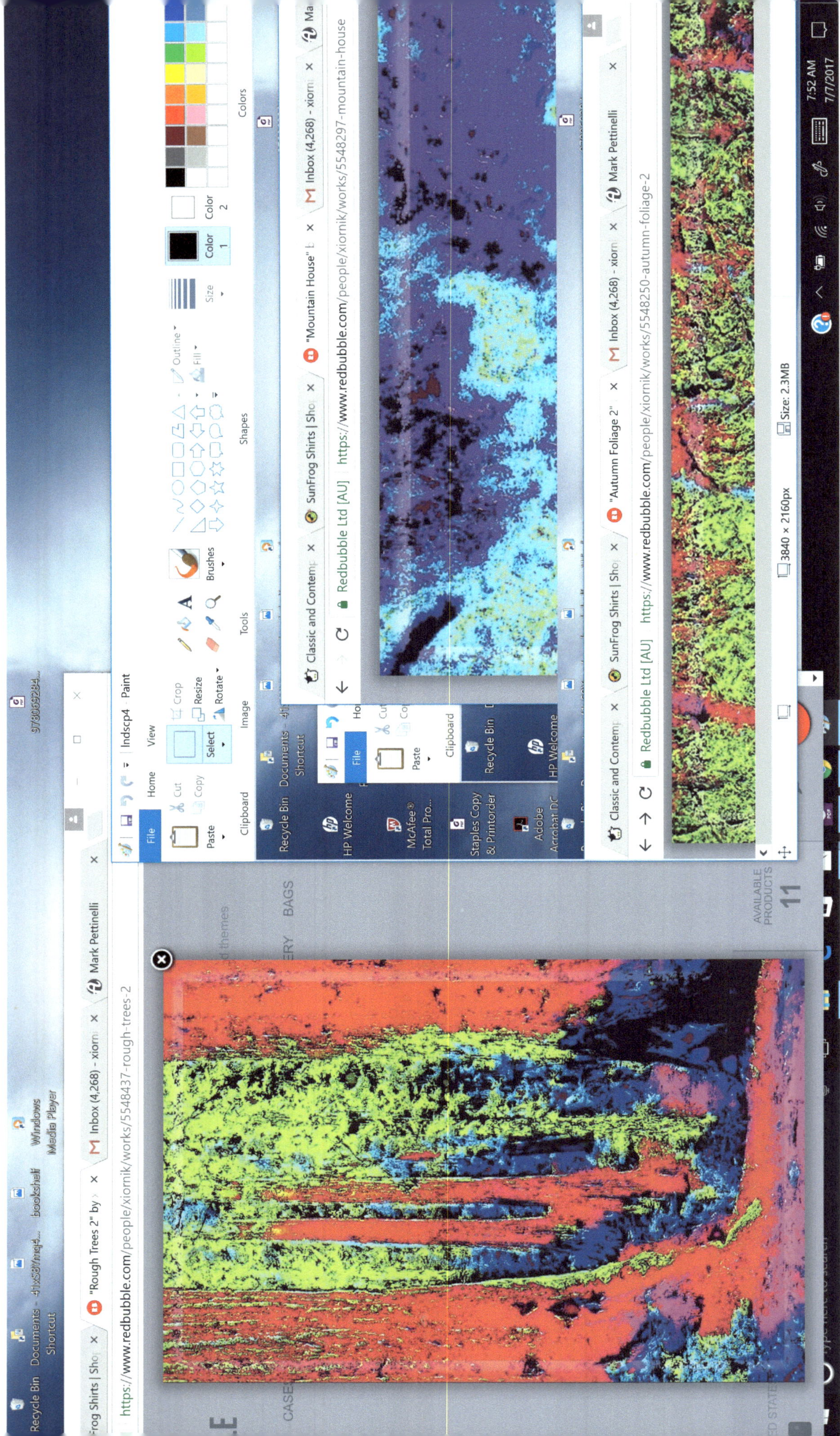

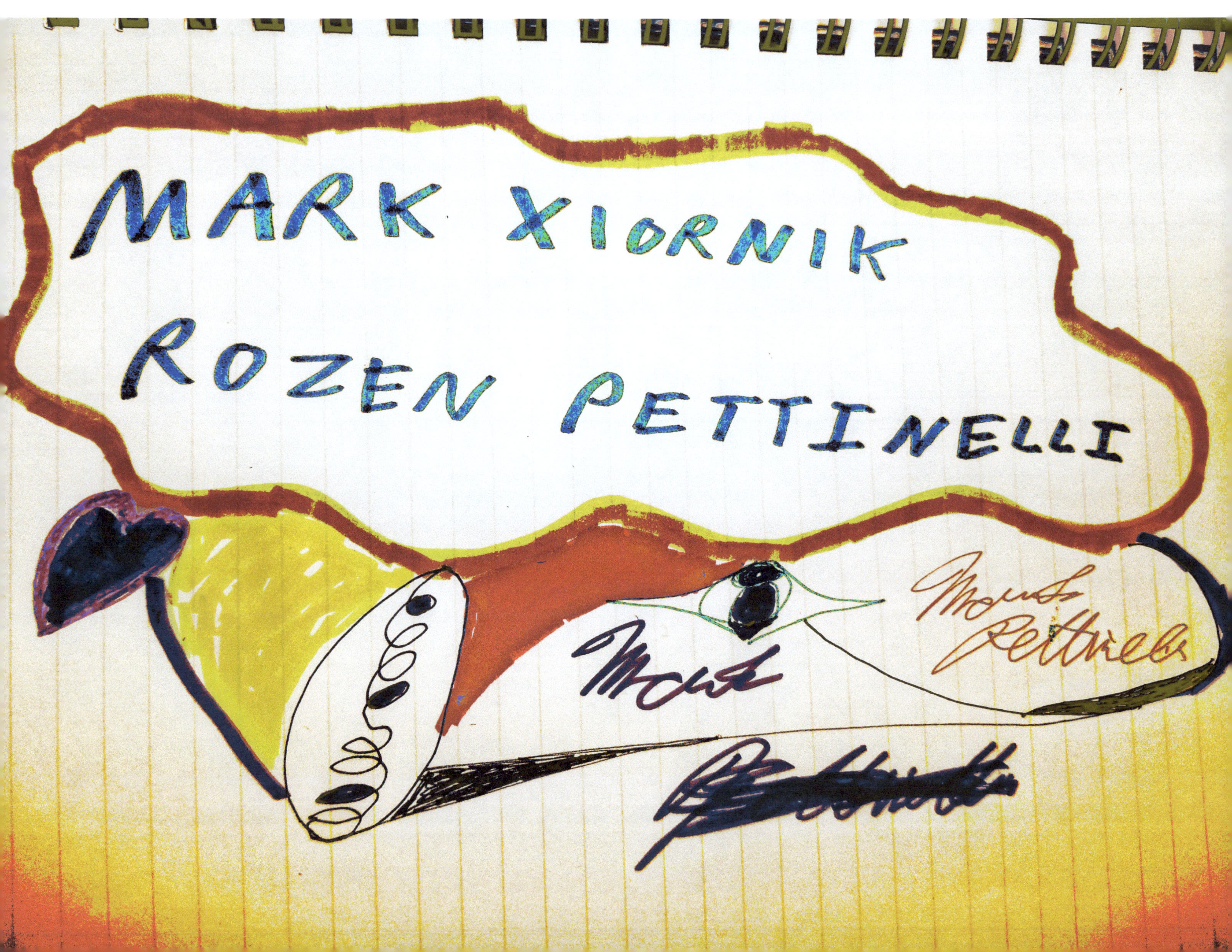

MARK XIORNIK
ROZEN PETTINELLI

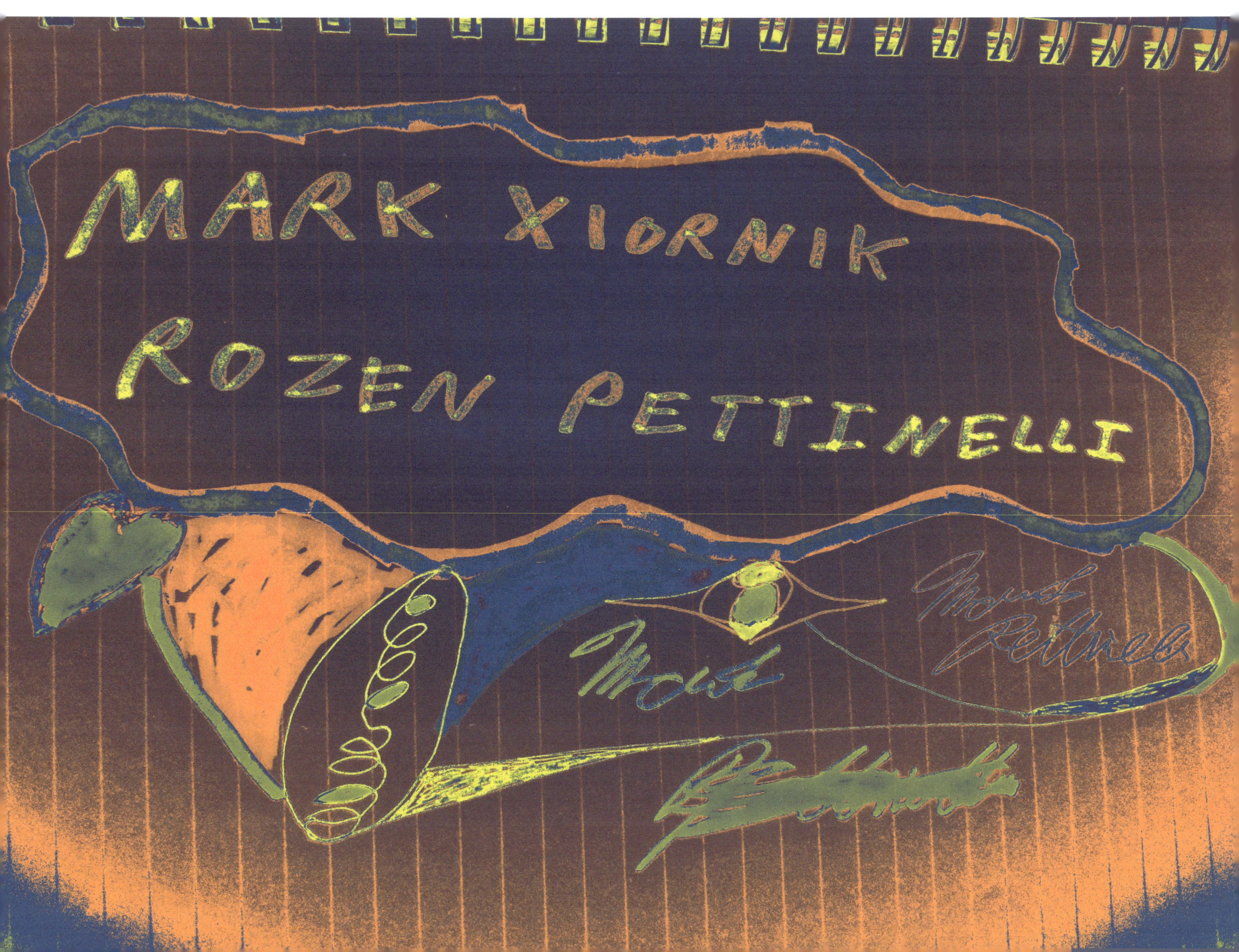

MARK XIORNIK ROZEN PETTINELLI

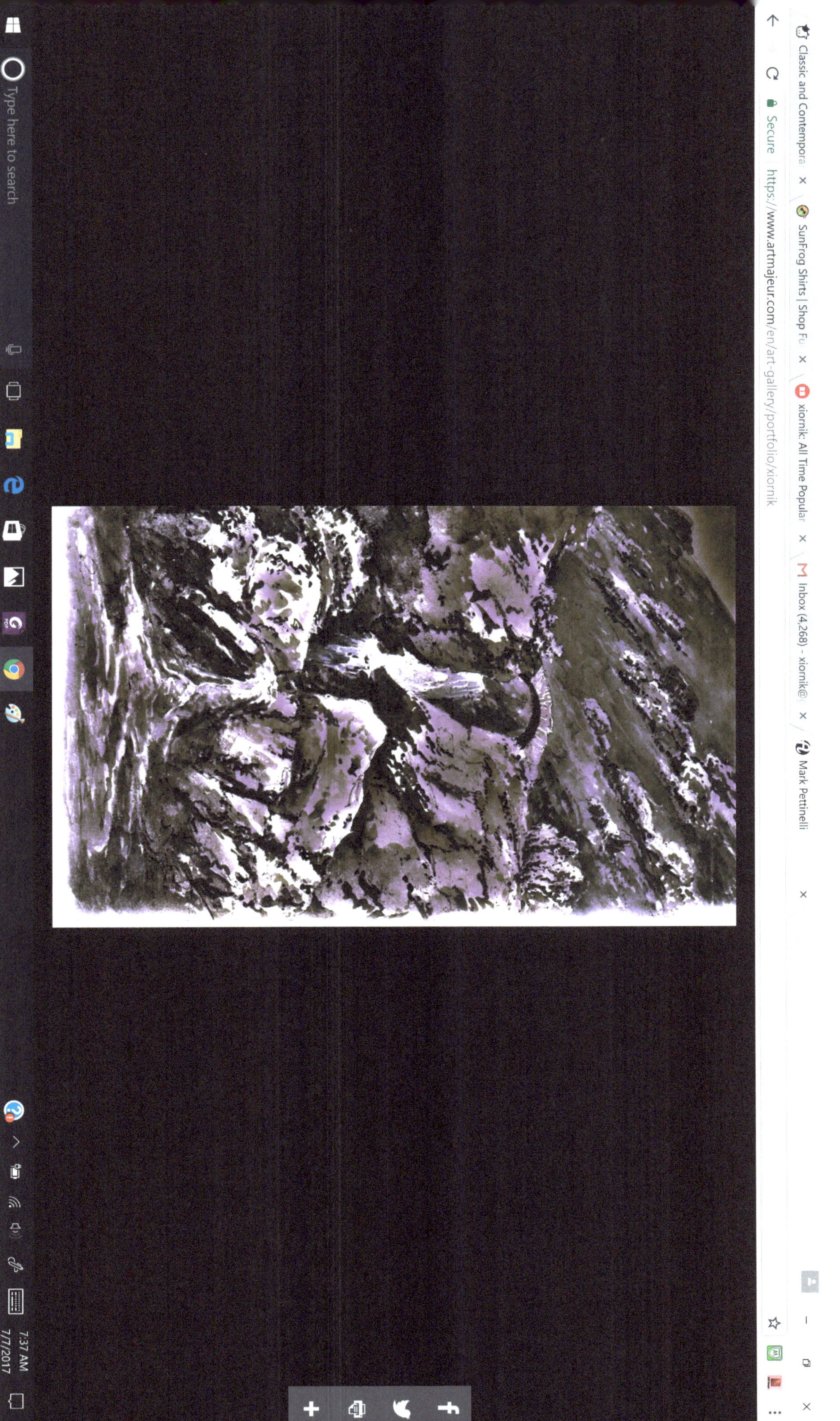

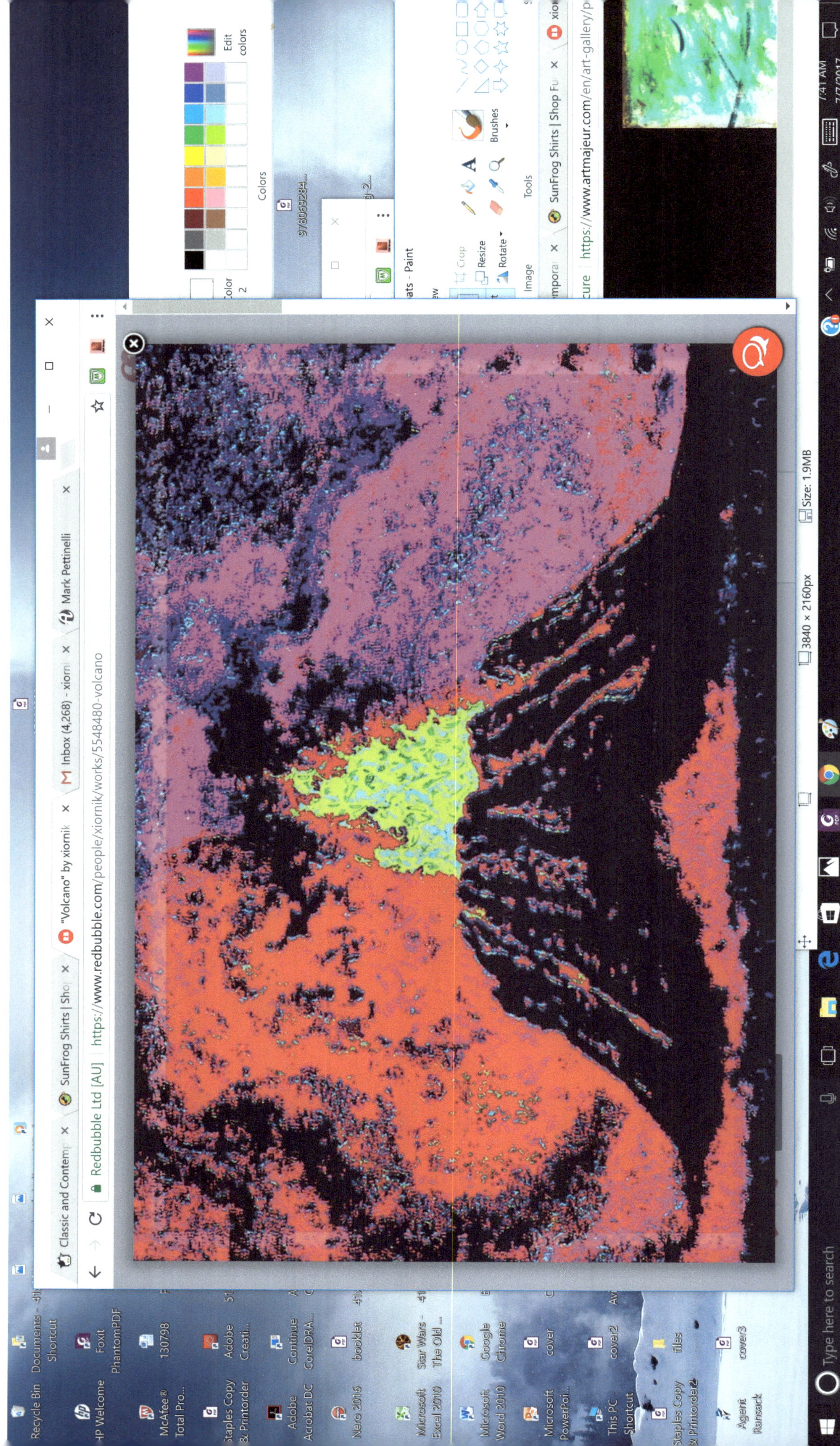

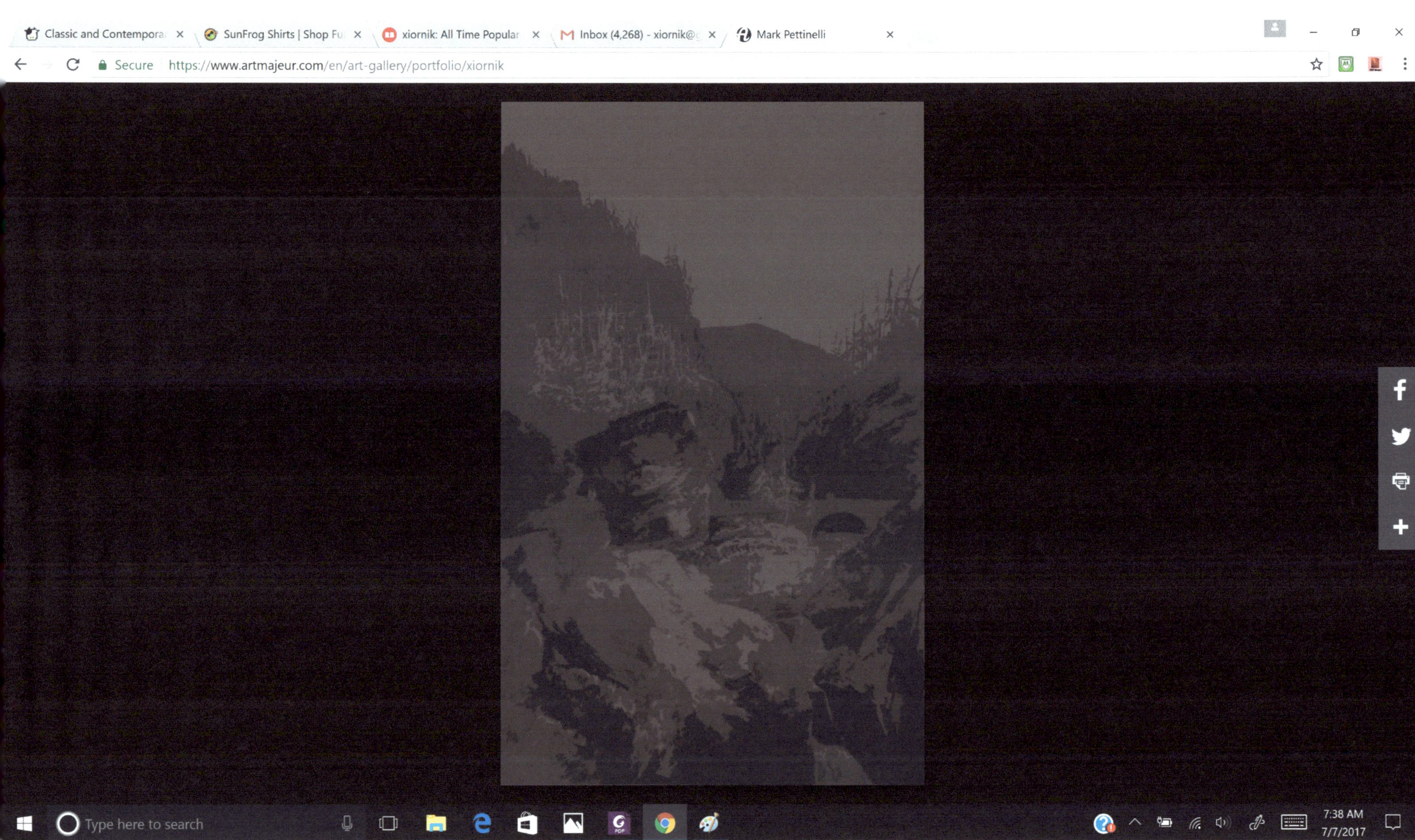
Classic and Contempora
SunFrog Shirts | Shop Fu
xiornik: All Time Popular
Inbox (4,268) - xiornik@
Mark Pettinelli
Secure   https://www.artmajeur.com/en/art-gallery/portfolio/xiornik
Type here to search
7:38 AM
7/7/2017

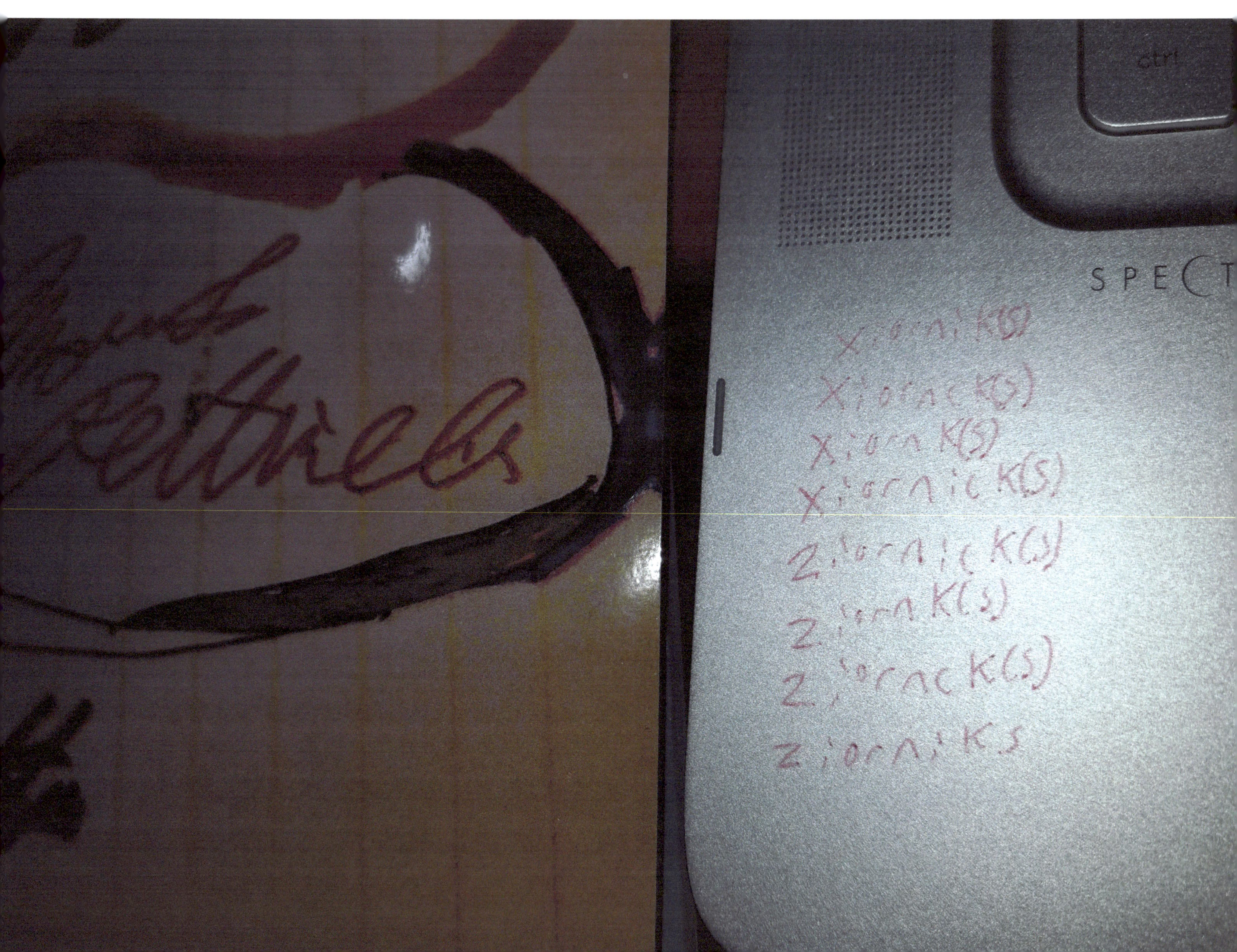

X;ornic(S)
X;ornac(S)
X;orn K(s)
X;ornic K(S)
Z;ornic K(s)
Z;orn K(s)
Z;ornac K(s)
Z;ornicks
SPECT
ctrl

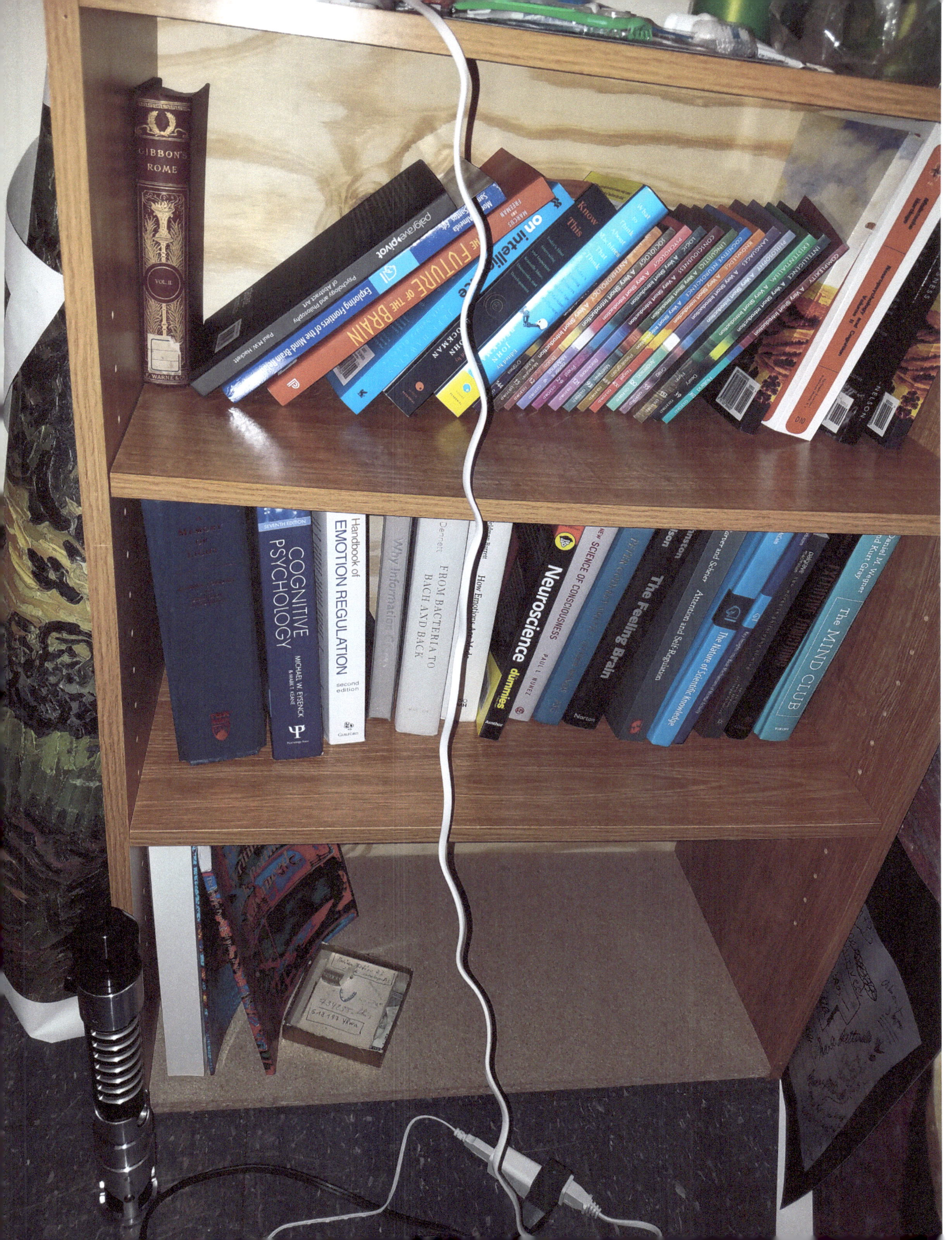

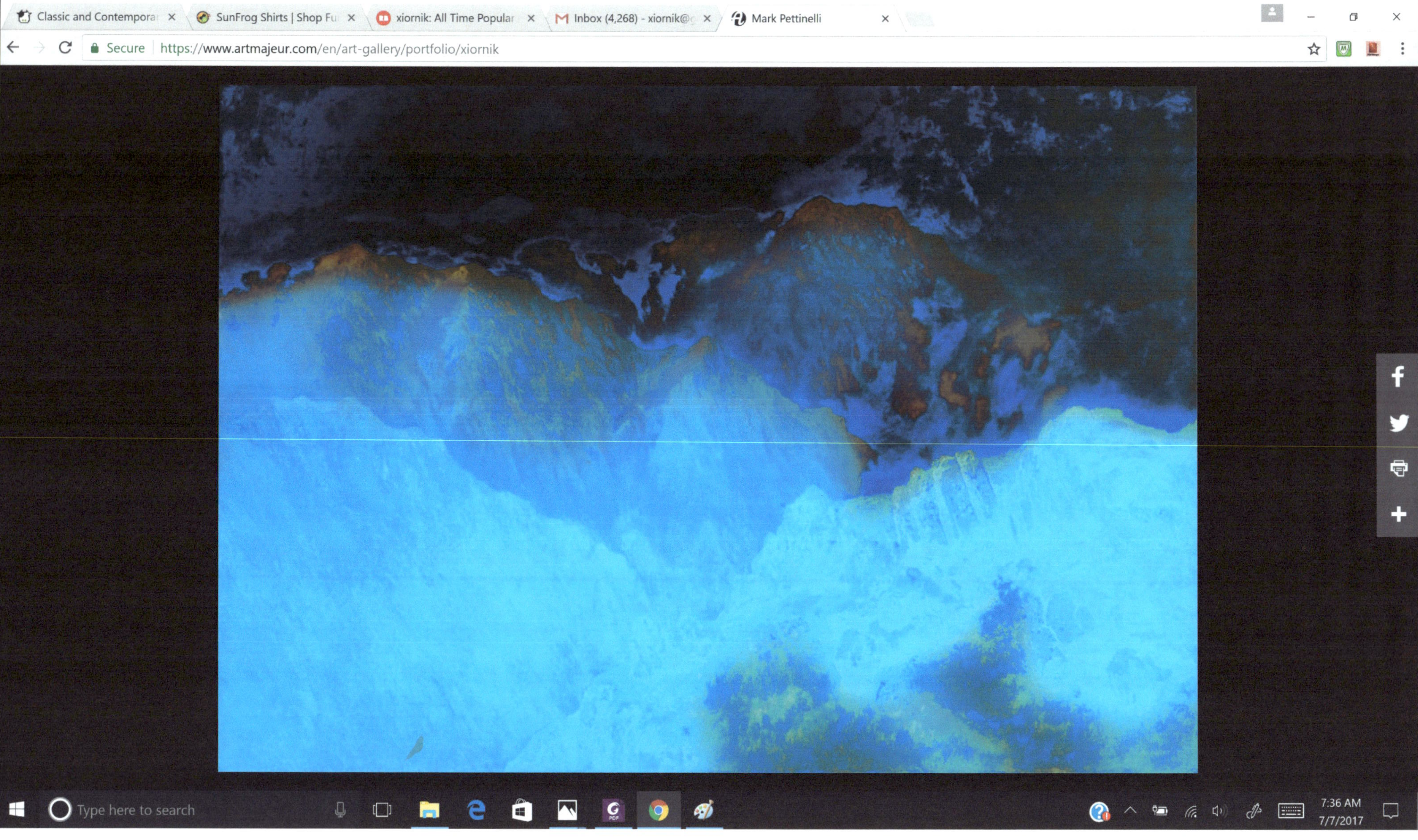

Classic and Contemporar
SunFrog Shirts | Shop Fu
xiornik: All Time Popular
Inbox (4,268) - xiornik@
Mark Pettinelli
Secure | https://www.artmajeur.com/en/art-gallery/portfolio/xiornik
Type here to search
7:36 AM
7/7/2017

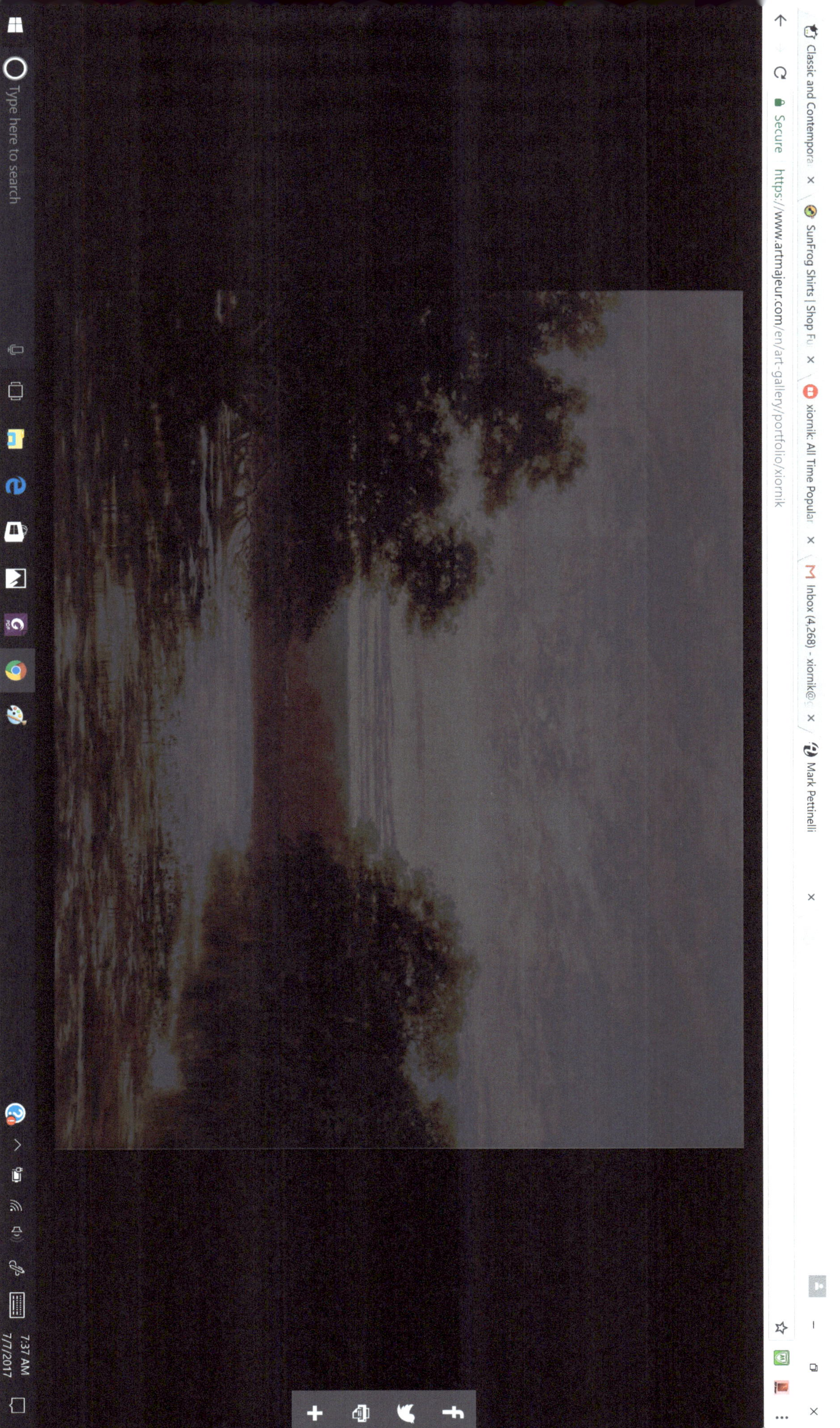

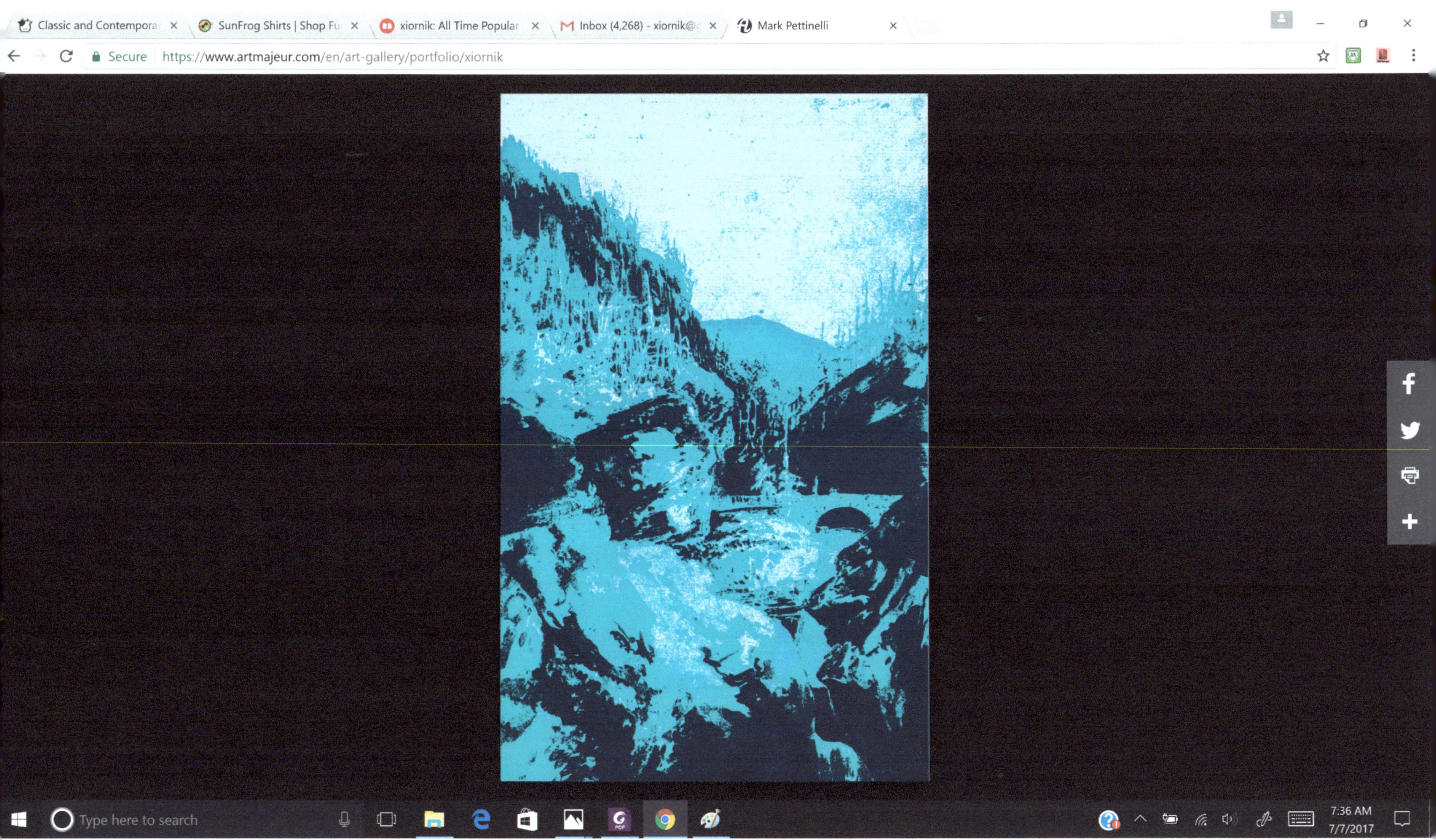
Classic and Contempora
SunFrog Shirts | Shop Fu
xiornik: All Time Popular
Inbox (4,268) - xiornik@
Mark Pettinelli
Secure | https://www.artmajeur.com/en/art-gallery/portfolio/xiornik
Type here to search
7:36 AM
7/7/2017

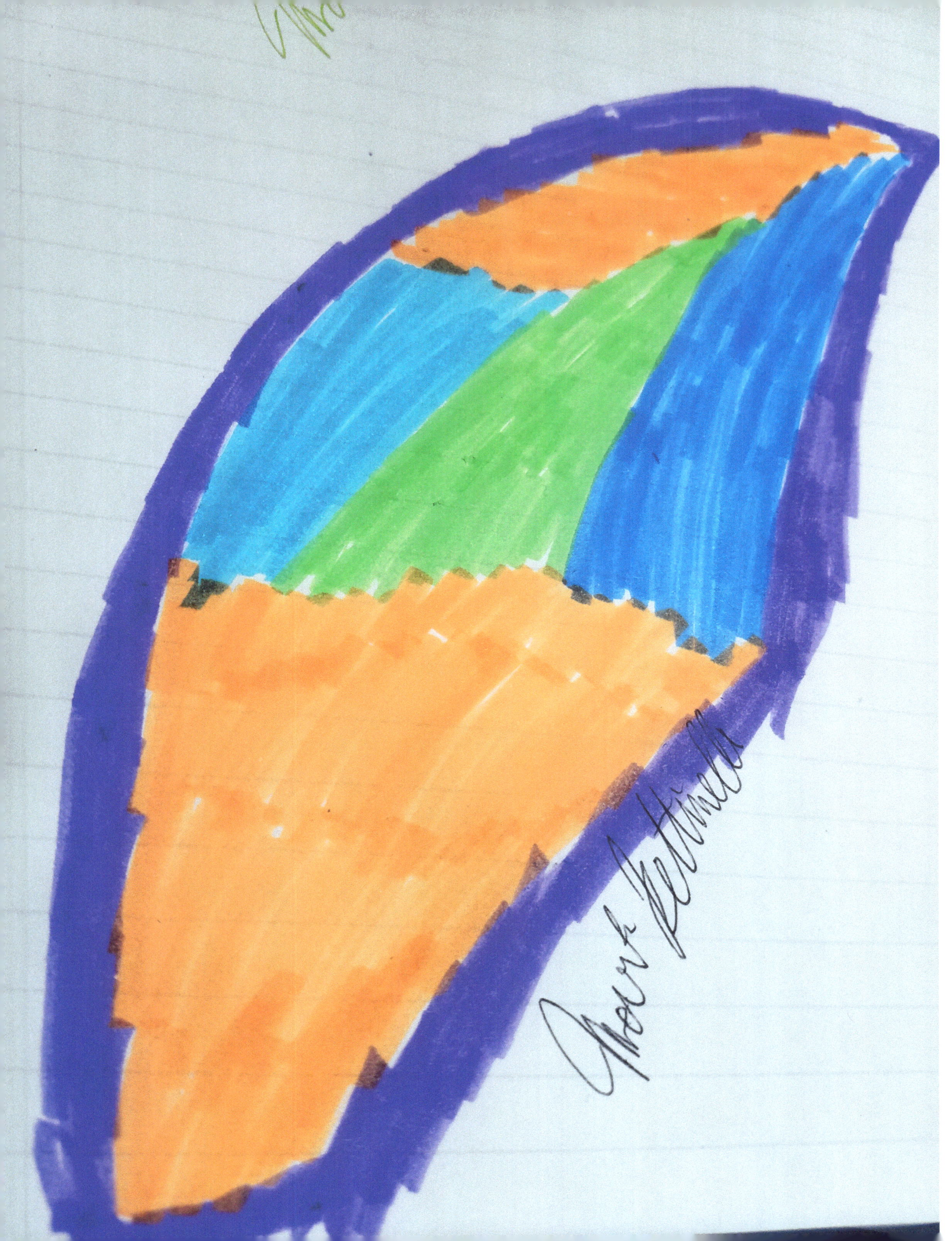

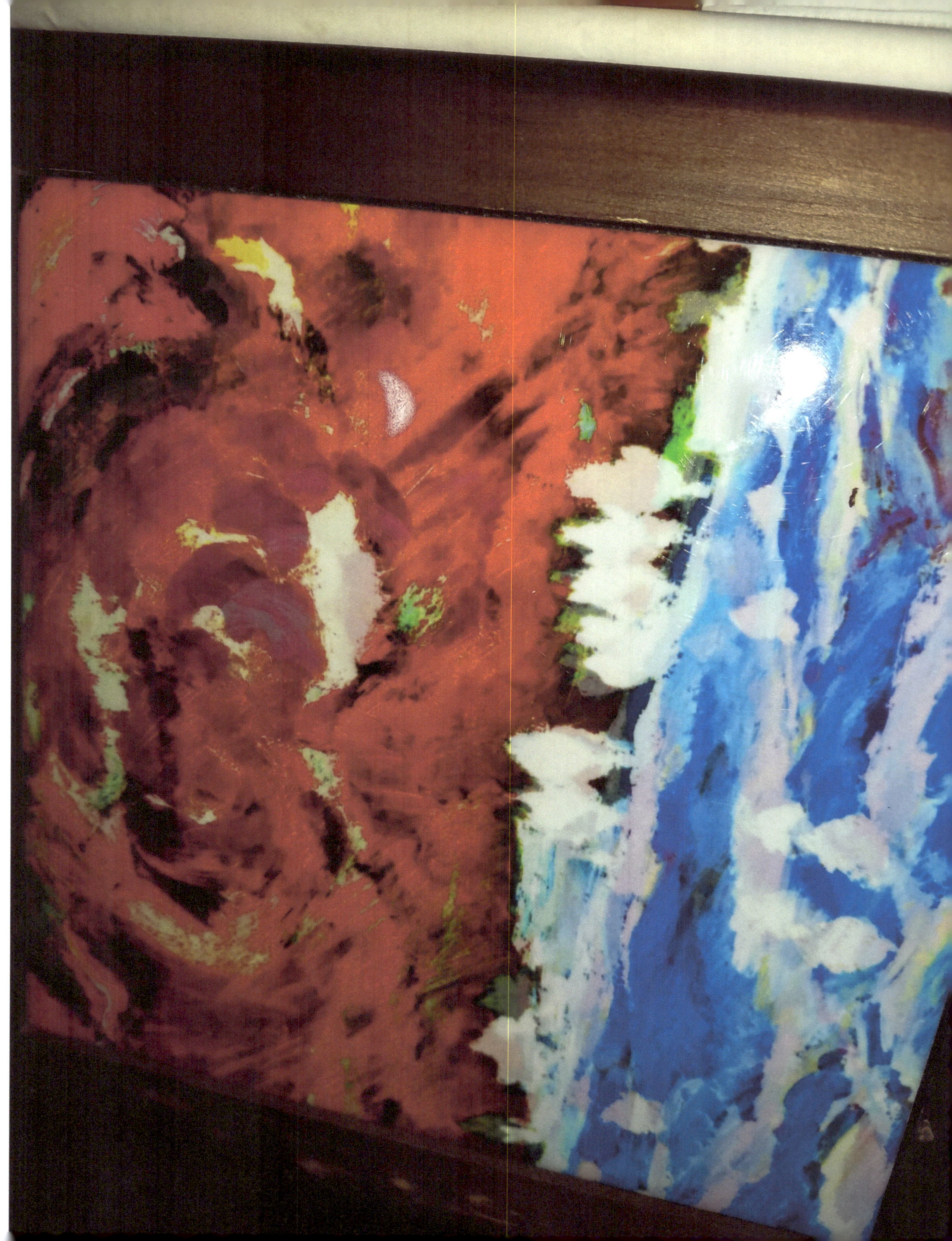

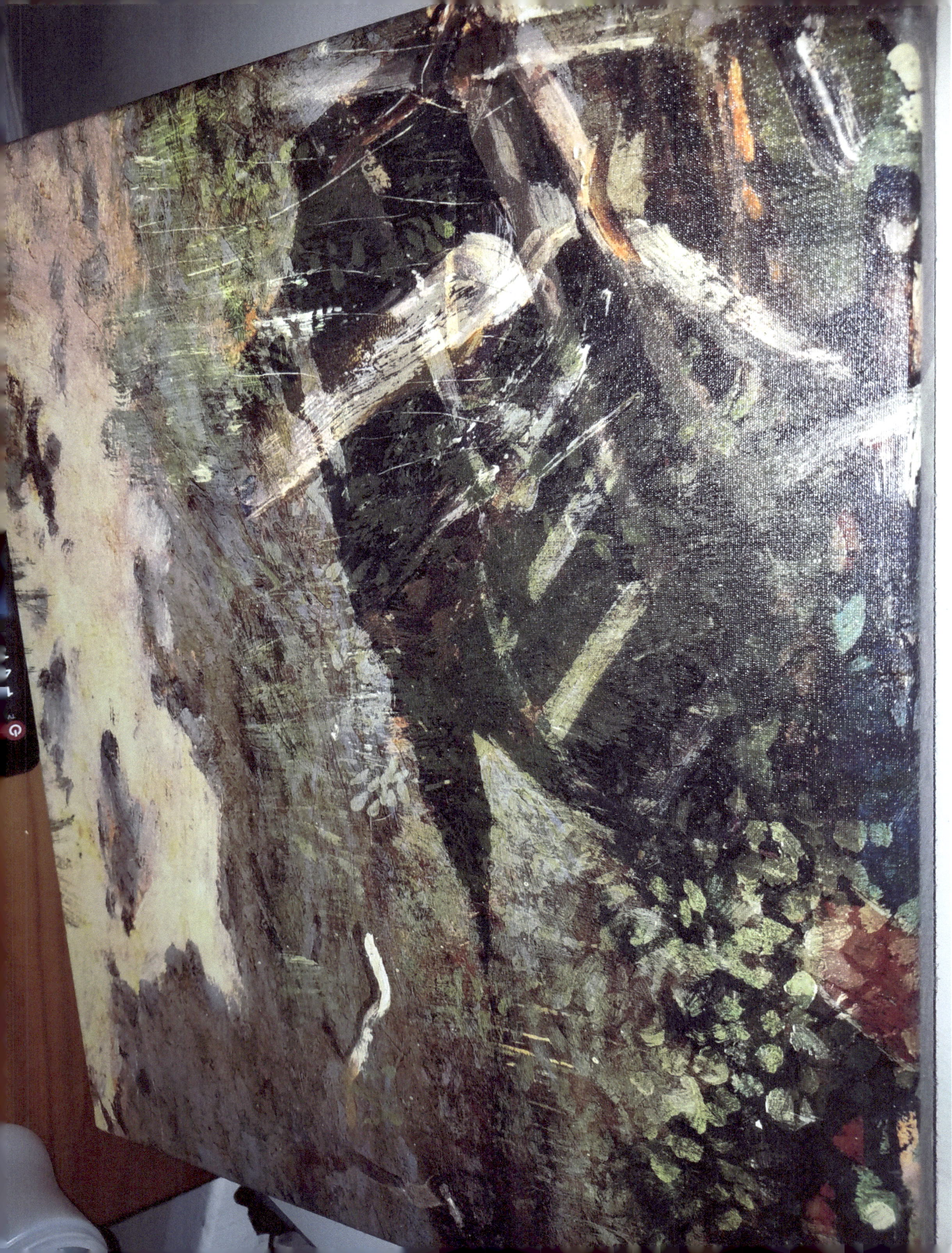

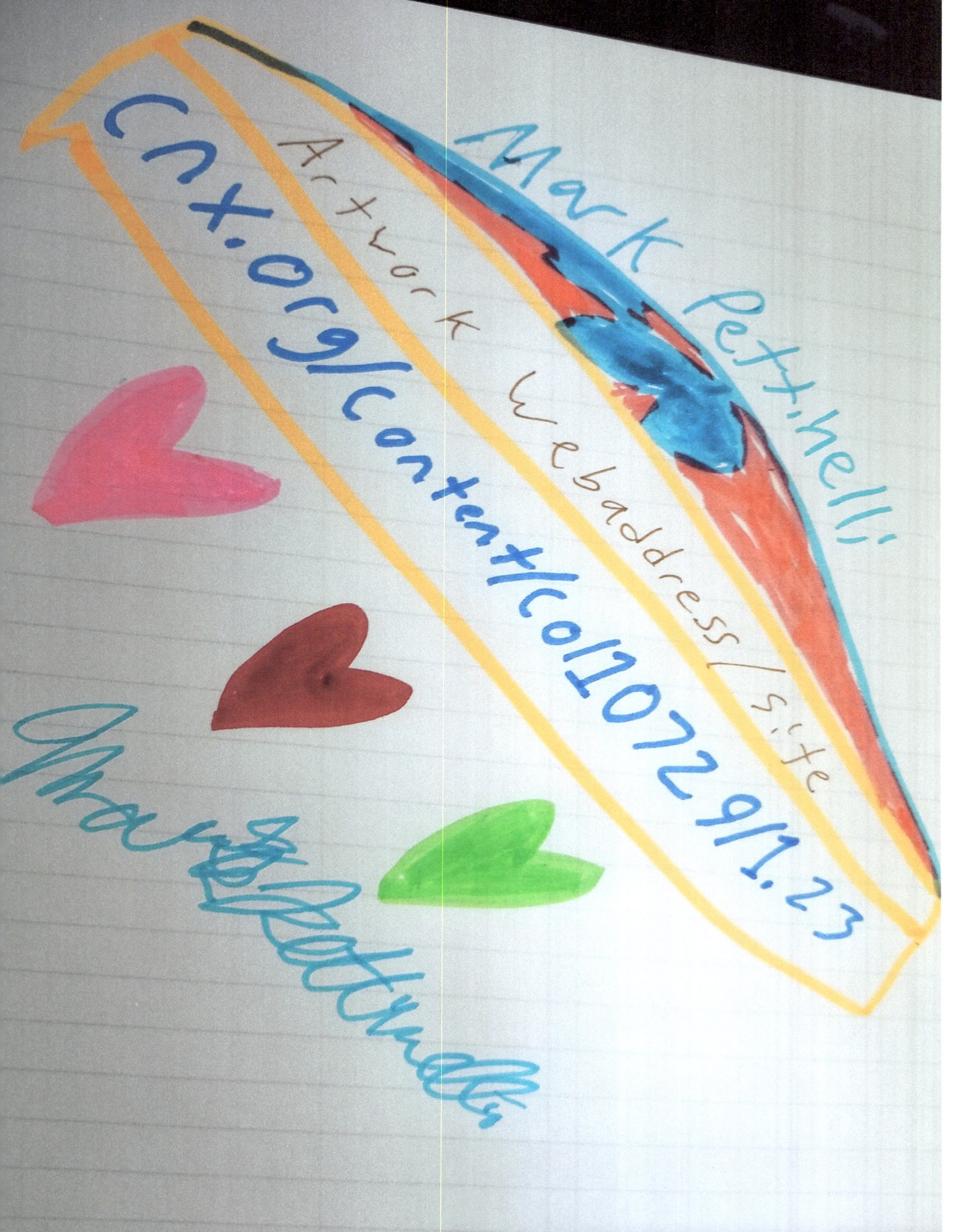

Mark Pettinelli
Artwork
Webaddress/site
cnx.org/content/col10729/1.23

Mark Xiornik Rozen Pettinelli Reviews Cognitive Psychology Research Articles[*]

Mark Pettinelli

This work is produced by OpenStax-CNX and licensed under the
Creative Commons Attribution License 4.0[†]

What is science or communication? Science is important because it is basically a rigorous or thorough understanding. What could someone achieve a thorough understanding of? If you think about it, if something needs to be communicated then you need to first understand it.

First something is thought about, then it is thought about more deeply, and then it is understood. That makes sense. If you think about it - when someone thinks about something for the first time a type of understanding dawns on them. This understanding takes a certain period of time to figure out, however. How long does it take for someone to figure something out? That is an interesting question, in order to figure out something someone might need to make sentences in their head or think about something with words. They might also make or think about sounds to themself - think the sentence out in their head with sounds, for instance. That process could enhance how the understanding of a certain concept is thought about or understood (figured out).

That is a good question, how exactly is something 'figured out'? It is probably more complicated than just saying the sentence of it to themselves in their heads. For instance if someone thinks about something with words then that can help them to understand something. However it isn't as if someone just says to themself, 'well if I think about it this way or that way, or if I think about this or that thing then I could understand this concept or idea better'.

Sometimes people need help understanding concepts or ideas from other people or influences in their environment. What kind of influence does other people have on humans understanding of concepts? Understanding concepts is important, what kind of idea is someone trying to understand? That is a good question, if you think about it logically then all the ideas in life can be sorted through and organized, and it could be figured out how difficult it is to understand each different idea.

How then would someone sort through all of the ideas in life and organize or categorize them? They could do it in various ways, I would think that they could it based upon which ideas are hard to understand, and also which ideas have similar physical objects - for instance you could label something physical an idea - say the idea of a 'house'. A house is a physical object.

Then would every word that there is in the English language, or in any language for that matter, be an idea? Every word in the language is an idea, and each word or idea also has a definition. That is, just like every word there is has a definition, every idea also has a definition.

Take the word 'I', the word "I" refers to the person who is saying the word, it means themself, "I" basically just means "me". That is an example of a word that has a definition. The definition of the word

[*]Version 1.29: Sep 10, 2017 3:59 am +0000
[†]http://creativecommons.org/licenses/by/4.0/

"I" is a person who is referring to themself. It is an idea, it is the concept of yourself or it is simply you referring to yourself.

Objects can be ideas

Similarly, any object can be an idea. Take the object of a house. "Houses" can be ideas just like they are objects. The idea of a house could be a place to live where you are happy, and the definition of a house could be a place to live where you can be happy, or sad, or any type of condition. The idea of a house is more selective, it is the idea of the house that is occurring to you at that time, while the definition of the house is similar, the definition of a house is place you can live with a certain type of condition or a certain type of house with various objects, while a different idea of a house could occur to different people. So basically different people could have different ideas of houses for themselves, while there would only be one good definition of a house that is descriptive.

That means that objects can be ideas. An object is anything in life that has a physical presence, and since you can think about anything in life that is physical, then it can be an idea in your head.

The idea you have in your head could be different from the object however. That is why certain objects are described as 'phallic' symbols, those objects basically represent penises. They are shaped elongated in real life, so in the persons mind they change them into the shape of a phallus (basically a penis).

That is probably the best example of how objects in real life have definitions, and they also can change when a person thinks about them, because they become ideas in the persons head.

Objects and ideas are important for defintions

This means that objects and ideas are important for a persons understand of a words definition. Also, not only do words have definitions, but since objects can be words, then objects also have definitions. I already said that an object in real life can be altered in a persons mind - how they think about that object is potentially different from what the object is like in real life, for instance.

If you think about it scientifically or objectively, everything in the world can be an individual object, and every individual object can be thought about in a persons mind. However, how the person thinks about objects often differs from what the object actually does in the real world.

Concepts are important for Comprehension

Understanding concepts is important for comprehension. For instance its important to understand ideas and concepts if someone wants to understand, well, what the idea is.

But what is it that someone is trying to understand? Is it the idea or is it the physical object or phenomena? There could be something physical that is present in real life that the person is trying to understand, say a house or the construction of a house could be a complicated thing that someone is trying to understand. Or, however, someone could be trying to understand what houses mean to them, like safety and a place to live. There are physical properties that could be understood with things or there could be mental concepts and ideas that could be comprehended with stuff.

My Digital Artwork Printed Book[1]

Collected Art Works[2]

Consciousness and Cognition Volume 52, Pages 1-124, July 2017

[MEDIA OBJECT][3]

That months' articles discusses memory and how it relates to vision and cognition.

If you think about it memory is going to relate to the other cognitive processes like vision and cognition. I mean, there are only so many cognitive processes - especially major ones. That might be subjective, however, depending upon how you would define a 'major' cognitive process.

---

[1] https://www.createspace.com/7335958

[2] http://cnx.org/content/col10729/1.21

[3] This media object is a downloadable file. Please view or download it at
<http://legacy.cnx.org/content/m64072/1.29/Gmail - Consciousness and Cognition_ Alert 09 June-16 June.pdf>

1 An Introduction to Ideas

There are many topics in education. Life can be described academically in different ways and can be categorized - for every category that life can be divided into there is also a way to describe that category (the material, stuff and ideas that make up that section of 'life').

What would be a simple way of organizing life or categorizing it? Psychology is the study of the mind or the study of life. There are also mental functions, humans perceive and feel their world around them. If you consider those factors - that humans perceive and interpret, and that there is material objects in the world around them, then the logical conclusion is that life primarily and fundamentally consists of humans observing the world.

Mark Pettinelli Northeastern University This assignment was prepared for course ENG 1105: College Writing I by Professors Barbara Ohrstrom; Justin Senter; Seth Stair 6/25/17
Working title: Can a categorization of different topics in Cognitive Psychology lead to a better understanding of the mind and categorization itself: can important information be sorted? Broad subject: Organize intellectual academic information in cognitive psychology and general academic categories (especially those related to the study of the mind) Thesis: Epistemology or the study of knowledge could be difficult or complex to study; in order to sort through important information someone would need to organize the different topics and the relevant information that falls under those headings/categories.

Buxbaum, Otto. (2016). Key Insights into Basic Mechanisms of Mental Activity. Springer International Publishing AG Switzerland.

This book discusses the mind and how it thinks – it describes how the mind uses judgements and concepts and memories to think in everyday activities. That is useful for this essay about figuring out how to sort through important information because the information that needs to be sorted is cognitive information in the mind. The mind itself sorts through information and this book talks about basic concepts the mind understands that helps it think like judgements, concepts and memories. Mental activity is discussed in the book and how it uses concepts and memory structures. In order to understand how the mind sorts through information it would need to be understood how the minds concepts and memory structures are formed.The book talks about mental activity and cognitive psychology, and while it tries to connect cognition and behavior I think that it is important to connect behavior to how information is sorted – since behavior (or action) is how information is gathered.

Sprevak, Mark and Kallestrup, Jesper (editors). (2014) New waves in philosophy of Mind. Palgrave Macmillan, England.

This book discusses, as is in the title, 'philosophy of mind'. Philosophy of mind is important to the study of intelligence and categorization because it includes a discussion of consciousness and intelligence. Intelligence is part of consciousness so thought, intellect and consciousness are discussed at length in the book. Those topics would help to advance the point of this essay which is to explain how minds categorize information – in order to understand how a mind categorizes information it is necessary to understand what it is like for someone to be conscious and to think. What it is like for someone to be conscious is described throughout the book. The book describes the material stuff about consciousness – called 'phenomenology' and the non-material stuff that is more mental and related to the concepts people use and what they think about.

Kevin Mccain. (2016). The Nature of Scientific Knowledge. Springer International Publishing AG Switzerland.

This book discusses, like the title of the book says – the 'nature' of scientific knowledge. It is important to understand what is scientific in learning material and any sort of understanding because it helps to make it more clear and, well, scientific. That relates to the point of this essay which is to clarify knowledge and figure out how the mind sorts through different types of information. If knowledge is scientific then does the mind figure out knowledge and information in a scientific fashion? The book talks about different ways to understand and figure out what makes certain types of information 'scientific'. What makes information clear and understood – that is a question that the book addresses. If information is understood then I wonder how the mind would 'understand' the information. Information is thought about in the mind differently from how it is discussed in public, for example.

Carver, Charles and Cheier, Michael. (2013) Attention and Self-Regulation: A Control-Theory Approach to Human Behavior. Springer International Publishing AG Switzerland.

The title of the book is 'attention and self-regulation' and it should be mentioned that by definition self-regulation is how the mind regulates itself, and when you combine attention with self-regulation then it is an implied understanding that it is how the mind works when it pays attention and thinks about regulating itself. The book is basically about the processes the mind uses when it focuses on itself, when it sorts through information that is within the persons own mind, for instance the book says it is about the 'self', and how the information in the mind gets sorted through. That obviously relates to the point of this essay because if someone is going to figure out how the mind sorts through information it needs to think about how it the mind pays attention and regulates itself.

Mark Pettinelli Problem/Solution Essay Northeastern University Author Note This essay was prepared for course ENG 1105: College Writing I by Professors Barbara Ohrstrom; Justin Senter; Seth Stair

The problem I've had since I graduated high school was basically boredom. I got anxious, high anxiety because I had nothing to do and tried to solve it by doing cognitive psychology and philosophy of mind research. I thought to myself that all the information in academics and life could be sorted and more easily understood, and in this way I could fix my mind and make myself think more clearly and be much less anxious.

I think that some of my problem had to do with what Tversky and Kahneman called "approximation and adjustment" (quoted from (Carver and Cheier (2013)):

A second judgement heuristic discussed by Tversky and Kahneman (1974) may be called "approximation and adjustment." This is the process of beginning an estimate by making a first approximation, and then reaching a final judgment by adjusting this approximation somewhat. The first approximation may be based on a partial computation (or partial decision), or it may be suggested by the form of the problem (or the decision being undertaken).

I basically kept thinking to myself the same thing over and over and that was part of the problem of figuring out how to think about logic and intelligence. I kept having to think about the same thing over and over, the same topic in academics, however I used 'approximation and adjustment' to think about what I was thinking. For instance, I had a topic in mind and thought about it, then thought about it a second time a little differently, and kept repeating this process throughout the day or week.

2 Problem of Boredom

So I basically solved my problem of boredom for the last decade (2006-2017) by thinking about cognitive psychology and philosophy of mind research.

I posted my results here on connexions (you can review my modules here) [MEDIA OBJECT][4] http://cnx.org/resources

Artwork PDFs

[MEDIA OBJECT][5]

[MEDIA OBJECT][6]

[MEDIA OBJECT][7]

[MEDIA OBJECT][8]

---

[4]This media object is a downloadable file. Please view or download it at
<http://legacy.cnx.org/content/m64072/1.29/XiornikPsychologyArticles.pdf>
[5]This media object is a downloadable file. Please view or download it at
<http://legacy.cnx.org/content/m64072/1.29/finalartworkpart1.pdf>
[6]This media object is a downloadable file. Please view or download it at
<http://legacy.cnx.org/content/m64072/1.29/finalartworkpart2.pdf>
[7]This media object is a downloadable file. Please view or download it at
<http://legacy.cnx.org/content/m64072/1.29/finalartworkpart3.pdf>
[8]This media object is a downloadable file. Please view or download it at
<http://legacy.cnx.org/content/m64072/1.29/finalartworkpart4.pdf>

3 What is the 'understood' part of Comprehension?

Insert paragraph text here.

This is a good question, what about understanding or comprehension is complicated or complex? It could be described neurologically, however most people would not understand the biological details involved. I wouldn't either. I could try to describe it in a simple fashion, or in a fashion that just involves the analog understanding. I will say what i mean by 'analog understanding' in the next paragraph.

Information can be understood, that is what could be understood - one could say that there is different types of information. Some information is analog, that is, it is made up of stuff - it doesn't have specific mathematical components, but is more like puddy.

That is good way that I can describe an understanding, it can be a mathematical understanding or a conceptual understanding. Conceptual understandings involve concepts and different types of information. Understandings that are analog do not necessarily involve any information but could just be descriptive or have stuff, have components that are not informative or not complex.

Analog by definition means not digital, so an analog understanding would be an understanding that does not necessarily have or not have information, but has stuff that can be manipulated non-digitally, like say with your hands.

Analog vs. Digital

I haven't used the terms 'analog' and 'digital' to apply to types of understanding, however they can be applied to types of information. However, since understanding stuff is understanding information then the terms analog and digital can be applies to the term 'understand' or 'comprehend'.

For instance when someone understands anything it is actually both digital and analog, it is digital because it consists of a set of information, and it is analog because it is made up of stuff, stuff in the persons mind and the stuff that the person is trying to understand.

So analog is anything that is not digital, that is not numerical. Numerical means that it consists of numbers. Or does that mean that it can be read and described with numbers? It could mean either I suppose.

That means that a digital watch is a watch with digits, and an analog clock is a clock with a hand instead of a digital watch with digits. That helps describe the difference between analog and digital.

4 What is Comprehension?

Comprehension is anything that is understood or figured out. Basically that means that there is a type of processing that the mind does whereby it understands different types of information (in life).

If the mind understands different kinds of information, then what are those categories of information? Off the top of my head I don't know all of them, however there are several obvious main categories of information in life such as foods, clothes, objects, buildings, streets and cars, nature, and art.

It depends how you want to describe the different topics in life, basically.

The different topics in life can be described depending on various values or definitions. Depending on what the person is trying to achieve or describe or define, in other words. I just described some categories based off of how I think a persons mind categorizes information for itself, that is one way to describe the different categories in life.

Categories in Life

Basically you can describe different categories in life. This is a good way to simplify how one thinks about things, if you think about it. In other words in order to think clearly someone might first need to categorize.

What might someone categorize? Furthermore, if someone wants to think with clarity (think clearly) then how would they go about organizing their minds with the proper information? I have some ideas of my own about how someone could do something like that. It was based off of my own thinking and how I have been thinking with my own mind.

Basically there can be different priorities, in other words the mind can think based upon different categorizations of information or priorities. Those priorities could be emotional and motivational or priorities about how they want to think about information, or what kinds of information they want to think about.

If you think about it, intelligent humans might want to think about information in addition to wanting to have emotions and ideas that they ponder and accept. Is that cognitive science and psychology? That is basically describing how the mind thinks and feels.

How does the mind think and feel?

That is a good question, how does the mind think and feel anyway? It depends on what the person is focusing on at any moment. If someone is only focusing on one thing, then that is the thing that they are thinking or feeling at that time.

However it is much more complicated than that I supposed, how would the mind organize itself to think and feel, if it wants to think and feel at any one time then?

It isn't as if the mind is a simple organ that simply feels basic feelings and thinks basic thoughts at any given time. The mind is complicated and it processes information and feelings in a complicated fashion. I would say that is accurate based off of the information of the minds many different functions, feelings and ideas.

Some of those ideas are motivations about the people around them or their environment, and some of the information that they think about could also be about their environment, or it could come from memories or previously learned ideas and thoughts.

Ideas and Thoughts can be Figured out

Different ideas and thoughts that occur to people can be figured out, basically. Sometimes those ideas or thoughts could be previously learned or simply take more time to figure out than instant ideas and thoughts that occur to them momentarily.

So I just mentioned that an idea or a thought could take different amounts of time to figure out. That means that it also is learned at some point. If an idea that someone has is an idea that takes them time to learn then it could be an old idea that learned a long (or brief) time ago. I would say there is a difference between previously learned ideas and previously learned emotions and feelings and new ideas, thoughts and feelings.

Humans think with concepts

Basically that means that people think with concepts. What is a concept then? Is it something that a person learns or thinks about? If you think about it, at any one time someone is thinking about information or processing feelings (or some combination of the two).

If you think about how many feelings a person has, and how many ideas they can think about, then they could be feeling a complicated set of feelings and thinking about (or processing) a lot of information at any one time.

What kind of description is that? I just said that humans have tons of feelings and can think about lots of stuff. Does that mean that they have a large capacity of feeling and thought or something?

How then does the mind process those feelings and thoughts? If you think about, its about input and output, and a central processor. The central processor is the mind, the input in the environment, and the output is their behavior and thoughts.

www.ingramcontent.com/pod-product-compliance
Lightning Source LLC
Chambersburg PA
CBHW042114030726
47599CB00002B/211